PATRICK MADRID

150
BIBLE VERSES
Every Catholic Should Know

SERVANT
BOOKS

PUBLISHED BY ST. ANTHONY MESSENGER PRESS
CINCINNATI, OHIO

RESCRIPT

In accord with the *Code of Canon Law*, I hereby grant my permission to publish *150 Bible Verses Every Catholic Should Know.*

Reverend Joseph R. Binzer
Vicar General
Archdiocese of Cincinnati
Cincinnati, Ohio
April 15, 2008

The permission to publish is a declaration that a book or pamphlet is considered to be free from doctrinal or moral error. It is not implied that those who have granted the permission to publish agree with the contents, opinions or statements expressed.

Cover and book design by Jennifer Tibbits
Cover image by Andrei Contiu/shutterstock.com

Library of Congress Cataloging-in-Publication Data

Madrid, Patrick, 1960-
   150 Bible verses every Catholic should know / Patrick Madrid.
      p. cm.
   Includes bibliographical references and index.
   ISBN 978-0-86716-902-7 (pbk. : alk. paper) 1. Bible—Criticism, interpretation, etc. 2. Bible—Quotations. 3. Catholic Church—Doctrines. I. Title.
   BS511.3.M326 2008
   220.6—dc22

                          2008016113

ISBN 978-0-86716-902-7
Copyright ©2008, Patrick Madrid. All rights reserved.
Published by Servant Books, an imprint of St. Anthony Messenger Press.
28 W. Liberty St.
Cincinnati, OH 45202
www.ServantBooks.org
Printed in the United States of America.
Printed on acid-free paper.
08 09 10 11 12 5 4 3 2 1

To Bishop Robert J. Baker and Father Bud Pelletier,
with deep gratitude. May God reward you.

—Tolle! Lege! —

TO SEARCH THE SCRIPTURES is a work most fair and most prof-itable for souls. For just as the tree planted by the streams of water (Psalm 1:3), so also the soul watered by the divine Scripture is enriched and gives fruit in its season—namely orthodox belief—and is adorned with evergreen leafage, I mean, actions pleasing to God.

For through the Holy Scriptures we are trained to action that is pleasing to God, and untroubled contemplation. For in these we find both exhortation to every virtue and dissuasion from every vice. If, there-fore, we are lovers of learning, we shall also be learned in many things. For by care and toil and the grace of God the Giver, all things are accom-plished. For every one that asks receives, and he that seeks finds, and to him that knocks it shall be opened *(Luke 11:10).*

So let us knock at that very fair garden of the Scriptures, so fra-grant and sweet and blooming, with its varied sounds of spiritual and divinely-inspired birds ringing all round our ears, laying hold of our hearts, comforting the mourner, pacifying the angry and filling him with joy everlasting....

But let us not knock carelessly but rather zealously and con-stantly... for thus it will be opened to us. If we read once or twice and do not understand what we read, let us not grow weary, but let us persist, let us talk much, let us enquire.... Let us draw of the foun-tain of the garden perennial and purest waters springing into life eter-nal (John 4:14). Here let us luxuriate, let us revel insatiate: for the Scriptures possess inexhaustible grace.

—Saint John of Damascus
On the Orthodox Faith, Book IV, 17

CONTENTS

ACKNOWLEDGMENTS

I'm very grateful to my wife, Nancy, for her loving patience and understanding while I wrote this book. My thanks also go to Robert Salmon and Ali Ghaffari for their kind assistance with the preparation of the text, to my fathers in the faith, Saint Augustine and Saint Thomas Aquinas, who, through their writings, helped me acquire rich new insights into Sacred Scripture, and to all those who so generously prayed for me as I worked on this project. Thank you, and may God reward you.

INTRODUCTION

There are thousands of excellent scriptural texts to choose from for inclusion in a book like this, so it's quite reasonable for the reader to wonder why this book explores these particular 150 passages, rather than a different group.

Part of the answer is that you have to start somewhere. It's no secret that although Catholics are exposed to a great deal of Scripture as it is proclaimed and preached on at Mass, many simply don't read the Bible on their own. And those who do typically don't read it in any systematic way. Consequently, most Catholics are at a loss to know where to locate specific Bible verses when the need arises, not just when a non–Catholic objects to some Catholic teaching and asks for biblical evidence in support of it, but for all manner of issues that arise in daily life that require the heavenly guidance one finds so beautifully presented in the pages of Scripture.

One of my goals in writing this book is to provide you with a particular set of passages that will help you through many key issues in your own life, much as they have helped me in mine. I wish I could have included many other important passages (the hardest part of writing this book was deciding what *not* to include), but I believe that these particular ones will get you off to a great start in your discovery (or rediscovery) of the vast, inexhaustible riches of Sacred Scripture.

It has been my experience that the 150 verses presented in this book are among the most important passages for daily prayer and devotions, making important life decisions wisely according to God's will for your life, dealing successfully with temptations, sorrows, setbacks and surprises, growing in holiness, consoling and counseling others and discussing your Catholic Faith with non-Catholics. We all need help in these areas. The 150 Scripture passages in this book will help illuminate the right path for you to travel when you come upon these important moments in your life.

I recently went on two back-to-back overseas trips. I was first in Japan and Korea for a week (fourteen hours ahead of the time zone where I live, in Columbus, Ohio). I came home for two days and left again for a week in France (which is six time zones in the *other* direction). As you might imagine, when I got back, my body clock was completely out of whack. A few nights later, I woke from a deep sleep and got up to use the bathroom. Groggy and disoriented from jet lag, I groped my way across my dark bedroom, not bothering to turn on the light. On the way back, thinking I was headed toward my bed, I veered off course and walked straight into an open doorway, hitting my face hard on the unforgiving wood and practically knocking myself out. I lay on the floor, dazed and in tremendous pain, with a gash in my forehead that bled profusely. An hour later, as an emergency room doctor stitched up my wound, I berated myself for being so stupid as to think I could walk safely, half-asleep, in the dark. It was a dumb move, and I had the stitches to prove it.

How does this relate to the Bible, you ask? The answer can be found in Psalm 119:105: "Your word is a lamp to my feet and a light to my path." You see, what I should have done was *turn on the light,* rather than trust in my own ability to get across a dark room while I was half-asleep. Just turning on the light—the simple flick of a switch—would have saved me a lot of headaches, if you will forgive the pun. We human beings are like that groggy, disoriented person trying to get from point A to point B in the dark. That's the basic condition we find ourselves in during this earthly life: surrounded by spiritual darkness. To make it through this life and safely into the next, we need a lamp for our feet, a light for our path. Happily, God has provided this for us in Sacred Scripture. We need only make use of it.

Jesus Christ is the "light of the world" (Matthew 4:16; John 1:1–9) who came to reveal the truth to us, to enlighten us with his saving gospel. To accomplish this, in addition to his own public ministry, Christ established the Catholic Church (Matthew 16:18–19) and entrusted it with the mission of taking the light of truth into the whole world (Matthew 28:19–20). God inspired the Old and New Testament authors to set forth his revelation in Sacred Scripture (2 Timothy 3:16) as a means of enabling the Church to fulfill her mission of carrying God's Word, both written and oral (2 Thessalonians 2:15), into the darkness of the world, illuminating it with the light of Christ. God has given us the Holy Bible to be a lamp to our feet and a light for our path. Which means that the more you read and meditate upon Sacred Scripture, the more clearly you will see the path ahead and the less likely you will be to collide with the many spiritual dangers that lurk in this present darkness through which we travel toward our heavenly homeland.

All of life's problems, worries, dangers, questions and uncertainties are addressed in some way—either directly or indirectly, implicitly or explicitly—in the pages of Scripture. With the Church there to help us rightly understand the authentic meaning of Scripture, you can rely on the Bible to be a light for your path. And since it's worse than foolish to stumble along in the dark when God's light of truth is so readily available to you, it only makes sense to take up that light and make use of it.

To make the best use of this book, you need only concentrate prayerfully and frequently on the Bible verses that follow. They are life-giving truth, the very Word of God expressed within the limitations of human language and set forth for our salvation (John 20:31) in the Sacra Pagina.

This book does not seek to provide a scholarly exegesis of these biblical texts. As you will see, I intend to comment only briefly on the Scripture passages contained in this book, wanting instead to draw your attention to what God himself says in his written Word. To paraphrase Saint John the Baptist's sentiment, "He must increase, and I must decrease" (see John 3:30).

Over the past 2,000 years, Catholic scholars have written volumes of profoundly insightful commentary on the Scripture passages you will encounter in these pages, but here I wish to simply introduce you to these verses, perhaps as new friends whom you are meeting face-to-face for the first time. Similarly, keep in mind that this book is not a work of apologetics (that is, defending the Faith). Although here and there it touches upon aspects of some passages that are particularly helpful in apologetics discussions, apologetics is not the aim of this book. So what, you might ask, *is* the goal here?

My fervent hope is that this book will serve you in three principle ways. First, I hope it helps you become intimately familiar with a wide range of scriptural texts—from Genesis to Revelation. This will help you in many ways, especially in more deeply understanding your Catholic beliefs and their scriptural foundations. It will help you "connect the dots" in some areas of the Faith that might seem opaque and difficult to understand. A deeper familiarity with the verses contained in this book will definitely help you understand your Catholic beliefs and their basis in Scripture more deeply, which will make you more confident and clear in your convictions.

Second, my goal in writing this book is to present you with an important sampling of verses (although 150 verses is just scratching the surface of the deep riches of Scripture!) that will provide you with answers to questions that will surely come your way. Sometimes, apologetics (that is, defending the Faith, see 1 Peter 3:15) is what's called for, and many of these verses contain truths that can help overcome objections and difficulties some people have with the Catholic Faith. Study these passages carefully and prayerfully, and I believe you will see a dramatic improvement in your ability to "contend for the faith which was once for all delivered to the saints" (Jude 3).

Third and most importantly, my hope is simply that this book will help you deepen your knowledge of and love for Jesus Christ. As Saint Jerome said, "Ignorance of the Scriptures is ignorance of Christ."[1] You can't, after all, love someone you don't know. So the more prayerfully you read Scripture, the more you will come to love it. The more you love Scripture, the deeper into it you will go. The deeper you go, the more clearly you will see Jesus Christ. The more clearly you see him, the more you will love him. And the more you love him, the more perfectly you will follow him.

—Patrick Madrid
Christmas, 2007

CHAPTER 1
The One True God

EXODUS 3:13–14

Then Moses said to God, "If I come to the sons of Israel and say to them, 'The God of your fathers has sent me to you,' and they ask me, 'What is his name?' what shall I say to them?" God said to Moses, "I AM WHO I AM." And he said, "Say this to the sons of Israel, 'I AM has sent me to you.'"

One can imagine how mystified Moses must have been as he knelt in awe before the burning bush and heard God reveal his name to be I AM WHO I AM. For one thing, that doesn't sound like a name, and for another, it is not easy to understand what it means.

Upon further reflection, it makes sense that God's name would tell us something very important about his nature. This name reveals that God is *he who is*. In other words, God doesn't simply exist; he *is* existence itself. All other things "live and move and have [their] being" in God (Acts 17:28).

The second of the commandments God gave to Moses was the prohibition against taking God's name in vain (see Exodus 20:7; Deuteronomy 5:11). Violating this commandment became one of the few sins that were punishable by stoning (see Leviticus 24:15–16). This helps us understand more clearly some things that happened to Christ during his public ministry.

In John 8:56–59 Jesus shocked and angered the Jews of his day by declaring that "before Abraham was I am." He used the divine name in a way that clearly showed he was claiming to *be* God. Many of the Jews in the audience, being zealous for the law of God and not realizing that Jesus Christ is God, took up stones to throw at him. In John 10:30–33, Christ again claimed divinity: "The Father and I are one." And again his audience reached for stones.

Of course, if Jesus had been a mere man, his words would have been blasphemy. He was telling the Jews a truth that they were not ready to hear. He was revealing himself to be true God and true man.[1]

Some non-Christian groups, such as Jehovah's Witnesses, deny the divinity of Christ, imagining him to be a kind of super-creature. If you should encounter someone who believes this error, be sure to point out Exodus 3:13–14 and how it relates to John 8:56–59. Those people who tried to stone Jesus understood him to mean that he was claiming to be God. And they understood him correctly.

PSALM 8:3–9

When I look at your heavens, the work of your fingers,
    the moon and the stars which you have established;
what is man that you are mindful of him,
    and the son of man that you care for him?
Yet you have made him little less than the angels,[2]
    and you have crowned him with glory and honor.
You have given him dominion over the works of your hands;
    you have put all things under his feet,
all sheep and oxen,
    and also the beasts of the field,
the birds of the air, and the fish of the sea,
    whatever passes along the paths of the sea.
O LORD, our Lord,
    how majestic is your name in all the earth!

When the Hubble Space Telescope was launched into orbit in 1990, it opened a breathtaking and mind-boggling view of the universe. This amazing piece of scientific equipment can detect objects that are *billions* of light years away from the earth.[3]

Now consider another scientific discovery: Looking inward, we see that our bodies, like all physical objects, are comprised of increasingly smaller particles (for example, molecules, atoms, protons, neutrons, electrons, leptons, quarks and so on). The "deeper" we go, the greater the relative distances between these infinitesimally tiny objects.

What's the point of these scientific matters, you ask? As Psalm 8:3–9 reminds us, God created human beings to enjoy an immensely privileged place in the cosmos. He has placed this incomprehensibly vast expanse of creation under our dominion (not tyranny). Not only should we fall to our knees with awe-filled gratitude to God for having created all this *for us*, but also we should never forget that everything in the created universe reflects his brilliant glory. His wisdom, power, beauty, truth, goodness and love radiate from each of his creatures. The heavens and earth and everything in them are, really and truly, a love letter from God, a reminder that he has something even *better* in store for those who love him (see 1 Corinthians 2:9).

Knowing this, doesn't sinful rebellion against his loving appear utterly ridiculous?

PSALM 139:1–4

O LORD, you have searched me and known me!
You know when I sit down and when I rise up;
    you discern my thoughts from afar.
You search out my path and my lying down,
    and are acquainted with all my ways.
Even before a word is on my tongue,
    behold, O LORD, you know it altogether.

Depending on your spiritual state, it will be either comforting or disconcerting to realize that almighty God knows all your thoughts, no matter how secret. Those who are in the state of grace have nothing to fear, but those who persist in a state of rebellion against God may cringe at the idea that God sees inside them.

Doesn't it make sense to live in the light of God's truth? How happy are they who throw open their hearts unreservedly and invite God to fill them with his light and peace and joy!

PROVERBS 3:5—7

Trust in the LORD with all your heart,
    and do not rely on your own insight.
In all your ways acknowledge him,
    and he will make straight your paths.
Be not wise in your own eyes;
    fear the LORD, and turn away from evil.

Humility is a very attractive virtue in a person. Saint Hildegard of Bingen (1098–1179), for example, classified it as the queen of virtues. This teaching from Proverbs is well worth memorizing and repeating often.

First, it reminds us that, while we may think we know what's best in a given situation, we might be wrong. (Just recall how often in your life you *have* been wrong!) And since God always knows what is right, it only makes sense to trust in his wisdom, not our own. After all, there is no comparison between his knowledge and ours. "There is a way which seems right to a man, but its end is the way to death" (Proverbs 16:25).

Second, this passage reminds us that by relying on God's wisdom and seeking his will, we are guaranteed his assistance. Those who trust in the Lord find solutions to the most complicated and vexing problems life can throw at them, often with miraculous ease.

Just ask the saints. Their lives are vivid testimonies to the truth that God provides astonishing, wonderful and seemingly impossible help, often out of the blue and at just the right moment. And one thing these holy men and women had in common was humility.

ISAIAH 12:2

Behold, God is my salvation;
   I will trust, and will not be afraid;
for the LORD GOD is my strength and my song,
   and he has become my salvation.

To paraphrase a popular saying, "Life comes at you fast. Pray hard." This earthly life is, for most of us, an unceasing blur of activity, commitments, errands, busywork and real work. There's very little "down time," and we tend to spend little of it alone with God. A person who watches two hours of television per day will watch for 730 hours in a single year, and that translates to an entire month spent vegetating night and day in front of the tube—talk about priorities being out of whack.

What's the solution? Well, it begins by taking seriously one of Scripture's most common themes: the steadfastness of God's love for us. He loves all creation, but he has a special love for human beings, as evidenced by the fact that he chose to become a *man* to save the human race and redeem the entire created order (see Romans 8:19–21).

It should come as no surprise then to see how Scripture abounds in promises such as Isaiah 12:2 above or Isaiah 41:10: "[F]ear not, for I am with you, be not dismayed, for I am your God; I will strengthen you, I will help you, I will uphold you with my victorious right hand."

When challenges arise, trust in the Lord. He loves you more than you can imagine.

ISAIAH 45:5–6

I am the LORD, and there is no other,
    besides me there is no God;
    I clothe you, though you do not know me,
that men may know, from the rising of the sun
    and from the west, that there is none besides me;
I am the LORD, and there is no other.

Years ago I had a conversation with a young man who had left the Catholic Church for Mormonism. His devout Catholic mother was beside herself with anguish, and she asked me to try to bring him to his senses.

I found this conversation sad because the young man accepted Mormonism's teaching that there are many gods.[4] This is so obviously contrary to God's revelation in Scripture, "There is no other." How could he be so deceived?[5]

Now, most of us are not attracted to polytheism. Yet it is well for us to ask, what are *my* false gods? What occupies my time, my thoughts? What motivates my actions?

Let's remember that there is only one God, and he alone deserves our total devotion.

MATTHEW 6:25–26

Therefore I tell you, do not be anxious about your life, what you shall eat or what you shall drink, nor about your body, what you shall put on. Is not life more than food, and the body more than clothing? Look at the birds of the air: they neither sow nor reap nor gather into barns, and yet your heavenly Father feeds them. Are you not of more value than they?

It's easy to become caught up in worry about things. Whether it's money or employment or some other real necessity, what

God is asking is that we trust in his generous providence. Matthew 7:7–11 reminds us:

> Ask, and it will be given you; seek, and you will find; knock, and it will be opened to you. For every one who asks receives, and he who seeks finds, and to him who knocks it will be opened. Or what man of you, if his son asks him for bread, will give him a stone? Or if he asks for a fish, will give him a serpent? If you then, who are evil, know how to give good gifts to your children, how much more will your Father who is in heaven give good things to those who ask him!

Watch very little children, and see how they rely on their parents for everything: what they eat, what they wear, protection from the elements—literally everything. And notice too how utterly *free from worry* little children are. They know that Mom and Dad will take care of things. That leaves them free to do what little children were created to do: grow, learn and enjoy life.

Can you see why Jesus said we must "become like children" (Matthew 18:3)? The fact is, childlike trust in God is the key to simplicity. And simplicity is the key to happiness. And true happiness is what God wants for you.

So be at peace and trust him. He loves you more than you can imagine, and he won't let you down.

EPHESIANS 1:3–6

Blessed be the God and Father of our Lord Jesus Christ, who has blessed us in Christ with every spiritual blessing in the heavenly places, even as he chose us in him before the foundation of the world, that we should be holy and blameless before him. He destined us in love to be his sons through Jesus Christ, according to the purpose of his will, to the praise of his glorious grace which he freely bestowed on us in the Beloved.

Like the rest of the Book of Ephesians, this passage's rich imagery of the Father's love for us is one every Catholic should commit to memory and pray often. The thought that God knew me from before the foundation of the world is, to use popular jargon, "mind blowing." God in his boundless love desires to make us his sons and daughters—not just on paper but really.

God showers on us the grace to love him and to be willing to be transformed. This takes us from being me-centered to being God-centered, from the flesh to the spirit, from the darkness of sin to the light of truth.

1 JOHN 3:1

See what love the Father has given us, that we should be called children of God; and so we are. The reason why the world does not know us is that it did not know him.

In heaven we will not just be with God, we will become more *like* him, as his sons and daughters. This simple but profoundly mysterious passage can be compared to what happens when a bar of iron is thrust into a furnace. Gradually the iron (human beings) begins to participate in the communicable attributes of the fire (God). The fire's glowing heat is imparted to the iron, which now glows white-hot because of its being in the presence of the fire. The iron does not cease to be what it is by nature, nor does the fire cease to be what it is by nature. The iron does not *become* fire, but it now participates at a very high level in certain aspects of the fire's nature. And so it will be with us in heaven, living in the immediate presence of God. We will then be fully, perfectly and forever his children to the fullest extent possible.

This process begins with our baptism. The more we immerse ourselves in God, the more we conform to his image.

REVELATION 19:9—10

And the angel said to me, "Write this: Blessed are those who are invited to the marriage supper of the Lamb." And he said to me, "These are true words of God." Then I fell down at his feet to worship him, but he said to me, "You must not do that! I am a fellow servant with you and your brethren who hold the testimony of Jesus. Worship God." For the testimony of Jesus is the spirit of prophecy.

Here we see an important warning against the sin of idolatry. It's difficult to imagine how Saint John, the Apostle "whom Jesus loved" (see John 13:20, 20:2), could do something so outlandish as fall down to worship an angel. The Greek word for "worship" here is *proskunéo*, the same verb Christ used in rebuking the devil: "Begone, Satan! for it is written, 'You shall worship the Lord your God and him only shall you serve'" (Matthew 4:10).

CHAPTER 2
Jesus Christ, True God and True Man

MATTHEW 11:28–30

Come to me, all who labor and are heavy laden, and I will give you rest. Take my yoke upon you, and learn from me; for I am gentle and lowly in heart, and you will find rest for your souls. For my yoke is easy, and my burden is light.

You know how, at the end of a long and tiring day, all you want to do is fall into bed and sleep? Well, that should give you a tiny sense of what Christ means here when he promises rest to all who come to him.

There are many cares in this world that press upon us: the dangers of body and soul that threaten us; life's disappointments, failures and tragedies; the loss of those we love; the keen sorrow, guilt and heavy heart we might feel over our sinful past; confusion, loneliness, depression; the fear, doubt, anger, helplessness and anxiety we experience over the turmoil we see in the world around us; times of sickness and even death itself. These are all aspects of what Christ means when he says so lovingly: "Come to me, all who...are heavy laden."

Christ wants to relieve your burden, soothe you, protect you and bring you in due time into the joyful and eternal rest of glory in the presence of the Blessed Trinity. All you have to do is, as he said, learn from him, and say, "Yes, Lord."

Why not close your eyes and tell him so, right now? Here's a beautiful prayer ascribed to Saint Ignatius of Loyola that will help you do just that:

O Christ Jesus,
when all is darkness
and we feel our weakness and helplessness,
give us the sense of Your presence,
Your love, and Your strength.
Help us to have perfect trust
in Your protecting love
and strengthening power,
so that nothing may frighten or worry us,
for, living close to You,
we shall see Your hand,
Your purpose, Your will through all things. Amen.

JOHN 1:1–5, 14

In the beginning was the Word, and the Word was with God, and the Word was God. He was in the beginning with God; all things were made through him, and without him was not anything made that was made. In him was life, and the life was the light of men. The light shines in the darkness, and the darkness has not overcome it.... And the Word became flesh and dwelt among us, full of grace and truth; we have beheld his glory, glory as of the only-begotten Son from the Father.

This passage—also known among scholars as the prologue of John—is perhaps one of the most luminously beautiful in the New Testament. In just a few words, Saint John unveils for us a penetrating glimpse into the profound mystery of the Incarnation of God the Son, the Second Person of the Blessed Trinity.[1] We see that Jesus is the *Word* of God who is *with* God and who *is* God.

Our time-based words fall far short of conveying the meaning of the eternal *now* that God possesses. We do the best we can when we say that from all eternity God has existed, and that there is no end to him, no point at which he "runs out."[2]

The eternal Word of God "became flesh" for our salvation, and this changed everything forever. The transcendent God has come very, *very* near to us. "We have heard,...we have seen with our eyes,...we have looked upon and touched with our hands...the word of life" (1 John 1:1).

JOHN 3:16–17

For God so loved the world that he gave his only-begotten Son, that whoever believes in him should not perish but have eternal life. For God sent the Son into the world, not to condemn the world, but that the world might be saved through him.

If you watch professional sporting events, you've likely seen someone in the stands holding a "JOHN 3:16" banner. God bless the people who display this important passage, because it's a succinct reminder that Jesus Christ is Lord and Savior. He came to save everyone who will accept the gracious gift of salvation—he won't force it on anyone—and he did this precisely because God loves us.

The next time you feel particularly unlovable, imagining perhaps that God doesn't even *like* you, open your Bible and read John 3:16–17 slowly and prayerfully. Never forget that God loves you so much that he was willing to come to earth and die for your sins.

I can't think of a better message to put on a banner at a football game, can you?

JOHN 14:6–7

Jesus said to him, "I am the way, and the truth, and the life; no one comes to the Father, but by me. If you had known me, you would have known my Father also; henceforth you know him and have seen him."

Christ repeatedly emphasized his being one with the Father. Not only does this verse help us see his divinity, but we also see his claim to be the unique Lord and Savior. In other words, there is no "Buddha" door or "Muhammad" door or any other door to heaven. The only way to God is through Christ.[3]

Furthermore, when one comes to Christ, he comes to know the truth, and he possesses life itself. This claim to be the way, the truth and the life is unique to Jesus Christ. He alone among all religious figures in history made such an audacious claim, and he alone did the equally audacious act of rising from the dead as proof that he was qualified, as God himself, to make such a claim.

JOHN 15:1–8

I am the true vine, and my Father is the vinedresser. Every branch of mine that bears no fruit, he takes away, and every branch that does bear fruit he prunes, that it may bear more fruit. You are already made clean by the word which I have spoken to you. Abide in me, and I in you. As the branch cannot bear fruit by itself, unless it abides in the vine, neither can you, unless you abide in me. I am the vine, you are the branches. He who abides in me, and I in him, he it is that bears much fruit, for apart from me you can do nothing. If a man does not abide in me, he is cast forth as a branch and withers; and the branches are gathered, thrown into the fire and burned. If you abide in me, and my words abide in you, ask whatever you will, and it shall be done for you. By this my Father is glorified, that you bear much fruit, and so prove to be my disciples.

There's a popular bumper sticker that reads, "Know Jesus, know peace. No Jesus, no peace." It's a helpful and catchy, if not theologically sophisticated, way of expressing the meaning of this passage. Christ is telling us that we must live in him, just as a branch lives only if it remains attached to the vine.

If you want to bear real spiritual fruit in your life—not cheap imitation fruit that quickly rots away—you must be united with Christ. We accomplish this (or rather, *he* accomplishes this in us) through prayer, the sacraments and good works of obedience to the gospel done in grace (see Ephesians 2:8–10).

JOHN 17:3

And this is eternal life, that they know you the only true God, and Jesus Christ whom you have sent.

In just twenty simple words, the Lord summarized the essence of his gospel. He wants us to *live*—in this life and for all eternity. And the way we receive the great gift of his life is to *know* the truth of God as revealed to us in and through the Son. If you know, love and serve the Lord, you have it all. When your earthly life draws to a close, he will bring you into the eternal life of heaven, where you will live in the presence of the Blessed Trinity, face-to-face, forever.

JOHN 19:28–30

After this Jesus, knowing that all was now finished, said (to fulfil the Scripture), "I thirst." A bowl full of vinegar stood there; so they put a sponge full of the vinegar on hyssop and held it to his mouth. When Jesus had received the vinegar, he said, "It is finished"; and he bowed his head and gave up his spirit.

These three English words, "It is finished" (Greek: *tetélestai*), convey an immense amount of theological information dealing with several major issues, including the passing away of the old covenant as it was perfected and fulfilled in the new covenant of Christ; the definitive atoning sacrifice of Christ as priest and victim for the redemption and salvation of the world (see Hebrews 4:15; 8; 9; 10); the completion of his public ministry and the inauguration of the era of the Catholic Church he established. It is a very good thing to pray before the crucifix and remember the Lord's words: "It is finished." He did it all— something that no human person has the capacity to do—and he did it for *you*. And now that the Lord has perfectly fulfilled and completed the eternal sacrifice for our salvation, it is time for you to enter into that spirit of sacrifice as a member of the body of Christ. Each time you assist at Mass, remember and meditate on those sacred last words of Christ: "It is finished." He spoke them for you.

JOHN 20:24–29

Now Thomas, one of the Twelve, called the Twin, was not with them when Jesus came. So the other disciples told him, "We have seen the Lord." But he said to them, "Unless I see in his hands the print of the nails, and place my finger in the mark of the nails, and place my hand in his side, I will not believe."

Eight days later, his disciples were again in the house, and Thomas was with them. The doors were shut, but Jesus came and stood among them, and said, "Peace be with you." Then he said to Thomas, "Put your finger here, and see my hands; and put out your hand, and place it in my side; do not be faithless, but believing." Thomas answered him, "My Lord and my God!" Jesus said to him, "You have believed because you have seen me. Blessed are those who have not seen and yet believe."

Among the many deep and important truths conveyed in this passage is yet another testimony to the divinity of Jesus Christ. Saint Thomas dropped to his knees in astonishment and declared to Christ, "My Lord and my God!" (It is salutary to whisper this mini-prayer reverently at the moment of consecration at Mass, by the way.)

Thomas definitely was not exclaiming this the way we might say, "Oh, my gosh!" That would have been clearly blasphemous—taking the name of the Lord in vain, a sin punishable in those days by stoning. Rather, Thomas was speaking directly *to* Jesus, whom he identified as God.

Jehovah's Witnesses, an aggressively proselytizing non-Christian sect that has appropriated much Christian terminology, denies that Jesus Christ is God. The next time any of their well-intentioned but seriously misguided proselytizers show up on your doorstep, tell them, "Jesus is my Lord *and* my God."

ROMANS 5:1—9

Therefore, since we are justified by faith, we have peace with God through our Lord Jesus Christ. Through him we have obtained access to this grace in which we stand, and we rejoice in our hope of sharing the glory of God. More than that, we rejoice in our sufferings, knowing that suffering produces endurance, and endurance produces character, and character produces hope, and hope does not disappoint us, because God's love has been poured into our hearts through the Holy Spirit which has been given to us.

While we were yet helpless, at the right time Christ died for the ungodly. Why, one will hardly die for a righteous man— though perhaps for a good man one will dare even to die. But God shows his love for us in that while we were yet sinners Christ died for us. Since, therefore, we are now justified by his blood, much more shall we be saved by him from the wrath of God.

The "mystery of faith" acclamation we say at Mass echoes this tremendously important passage: "Dying, you destroyed our

death; rising, you restored our life; Lord Jesus, come in glory."
Christ, who is sinless and innocent, died for us guilty sinners
because of his love for us. His death conquered death; he died
so that we might live. His Resurrection demonstrated that he
had accomplished our redemption.

This is why we have hope. We know that, as Saint Paul
says, we will not be disappointed.

1 CORINTHIANS 1:18–23

For the word of the cross is folly to those who are perish-
ing, but to us who are being saved it is the power of God.
For it is written,

> "I will destroy the wisdom of the wise,
> and the cleverness of the clever I will thwart."

Where is the wise man? Where is the scribe? Where is the
debater of this age? Has not God made foolish the wisdom
of the world? For since, in the wisdom of God, the world
did not know God through wisdom, it pleased God through
the folly of what we preach to save those who believe. For
Jews demand signs and Greeks seek wisdom, but we preach
Christ crucified, a stumbling block to Jews and folly to
Gentiles.

Have you noticed that when you see an empty cross, your
mind immediately thinks of Christ's death on the cross? The
reason is that the *meaning* of the cross is the crucifixion. The
Lord's supreme sacrifice of atonement for us was accomplished
there. An empty cross simply points to the reality of the crucifixion, and apart from it, a cross has no intrinsic religious
meaning.

For this reason Saint Paul's comments about "preaching
Christ crucified" in this passage (see also 1 Corinthians 2:2) are
very helpful when explaining to non-Catholics why Catholics

have crucifixes as well as plain crosses. (The difference is that the crucifix depicts the body of Christ crucified, while a cross has no "corpus.") For some, the Catholic crucifix seems tantamount to "keeping Christ on the cross," as if that meant we don't think he suffered enough or some such thing. This, of course, is not the case.

Saint Paul was a Catholic. It makes perfect sense, therefore, that the Catholic Church would continue to proclaim his message of "Christ crucified," not being swayed by those who are, for one reason or another, offended by the crucifix and whose negative attitude toward it echoes the shouts of "Come down off your cross!" (Mark 15:30) from some who gathered on Golgotha that dark afternoon.

GALATIANS 2:19-20

For I through the law died to the law, that I might live to God. I have been crucified with Christ; it is no longer I who live, but Christ who lives in me; and the life I now live in the flesh I live by faith in the Son of God, who loved me and gave himself for me.

Sometimes verses we've read many times will suddenly rise off the sacred page, riveting our attention and making us think. Thank you, Lord, for the power of your grace in the pages of your written Word!

Think for a while about these words: *Christ loved me and gave himself for me*. This means that Christ offered his life for you—for all of us—out of love. What kind of burning, yearning love must possess the Second Person of the Trinity, God himself, to condescend to take on flesh to save us!

Sacred art offers innumerable depictions of the excruciating sufferings that Jesus endured for us. How can we not love him in return? How can we crucify him again, spit and jeer at him, which is what we do each time we choose to sin instead of follow him? It makes no sense.

Pray:

Lord Jesus, please forgive me for all the times I forget how much you love me and how much you suffered on my behalf. How often I take your love for granted! For the times that I spurn your love by my wickedness, forgive me, O Lord.

COLOSSIANS 1:15—20

He is the image of the invisible God, the first-born of all creation; for in him all things were created, in heaven and on earth, visible and invisible, whether thrones or dominions or principalities or authorities—all things were created through him and for him. He is before all things, and in him all things hold together. He is the head of the body, the Church; he is the beginning, the first-born from the dead, that in everything he might be pre-eminent. For in him all the fullness of God was pleased to dwell, and through him to reconcile to himself all things, whether on earth or in heaven, making peace by the blood of his cross.

This luminous passage is among the most important Christological texts in all of Scripture. Several key things are revealed to us here, which I will only briefly identify.

First, Christ is the *image* of the Father.[4] This is incarnational language, reminiscent of how a royal signet ring impresses its image into hot wax. Christ is true God and true man. We see here that God creates the cosmos through the Son, the Second Person of the Trinity. The fullness of the Godhead is present in this (and all) divine acts, but creation is shown here as being effected through the Son.[5] The mystery of the Incarnation—Jesus Christ is true God and true man, existing beyond time and yet in time—is unveiled somewhat for us here. He is higher than all the angels, having created them all (see Hebrews 1:1–14).

Second, as Head of the Church, all members of Christ's body enjoy an organic unity, both with him and with all the other members of the body (see 1 Corinthians 12:12–27). Third, the *fullness* of divinity is in Christ. This means that in no way, according to his divine nature, is he less than or inferior to the Father. His humanity, of course, is a creature, which explains why we encounter some passages that speak of the Father being "greater" than the Son. And finally, Jesus Christ is the unique redeemer of the world. Salvation comes through him alone (see Acts 4:12).

HEBREWS 4:12–13

For the word of God is living and active, sharper than any two-edged sword, piercing to the division of soul and spirit, of joints and marrow, and discerning the thoughts and intentions of the heart. And before him no creature is hidden, but all are open and laid bare to the eyes of him with whom we have to do.

The "Word of God" mentioned in this passage is not the Bible; it is Christ. This might seem like a minor or even unimportant piece of information, but it has important ramifications on discussions about authority between Catholics and Protestants. Very often Hebrews 4 is misunderstood to mean that the Bible itself is active and living and discerning our thoughts. Rather, as the last part of the verse shows, it is referring to Christ, to whom we will all one day give an account of our lives (see Matthew 25:31–46).

CHAPTER 3
Salvation

ISAIAH 55:6—9

Seek the LORD while he may be found,
    call upon him while he is near;
let the wicked forsake his way,
    and the unrighteous man his thoughts;
let him return to the LORD, that he may have mercy on him,
    and to our God, for he will abundantly pardon.
For my thoughts are not your thoughts,
    neither are your ways my ways, says the LORD.
For as the heavens are higher than the earth,
    so are my ways higher than your ways
    and my thoughts than your thoughts.

There are several hugely important truths contained in this brief passage.

First, God is reminding us of the urgency of repenting, of turning to him and away from sin. This is precisely what the word *conversion* means: to turn away from something (sin) and toward something else (God). The reason for the urgency— "Seek the Lord *while he may be found...while he is near*"—is that, sooner or later, whether we like it or not, it will be too late to turn to God. That time is known as the particular judgment, which each human being experiences at the end of his or her life (see Hebrews 9:27). The time of God's mercy is during this earthly life, so take advantage of his mercy now.

The U.S. Census Bureau estimates that the annual global death rate is about fifty-five million.[1] Many of these deaths are sudden. Car crashes and other accidents, strokes, heart attacks and so on, take many by surprise. The lesson is, be prepared.

The second major truth here is that God *wants* to pardon you (see Romans 2:4). He loves you more than you love yourself— vastly, incomprehensibly more—and he's extending his mercy to you without limitation every second of your earthly life.

Many Catholics labor under the dark fear that God is some- how out to get them, that he really doesn't *like* them all that much, and that he's just waiting for opportunities to zap them.[2] Not true. It's worth repeating that God *loves* you. Yes, he surely does hate your *sins*, but that's because they turn you away from him and create barriers of selfishness and hard-heartedness between you and him.

This is the essence of Christ's Divine Mercy revelations in the 1930s to Saint Faustina Kowalska and the revelations of his Sacred Heart in the seventeenth century to Saint Margaret Mary Alacoque. In these apparitions Christ emphasized his tremen- dous love for us and his desire that we trust in that love.

The third major truth contained in this passage is that God's ways are infinitely above ours. We're often at a loss to comprehend why God would allow terrible things like earth- quakes, plane crashes and abortions.[3] God is telling us to "chill out," to not get worked up over the fact that we don't under- stand his decisions. Praying as the Lord taught Saint Faustina, "Jesus, I trust in you," will yield rich dividends.

MATTHEW 6:1–4

Beware of practicing your piety before men in order to be seen by them; for then you will have no reward from your Father who is in heaven.

Thus, when you give alms, sound no trumpet before you, as the hypocrites do in the synagogues and in the streets, that they may be praised by men. Truly, I say to you, they have their reward. But when you give alms, do not let your left

hand know what your right hand is doing, so that your alms
may be in secret; and your Father who sees in secret will
reward you.

No one likes a hypocrite, and God is no exception. Here he is
telling us that our external actions of piety must be *authentic*,
not contrived; heartfelt and selfless, not calculated for some
earthly gain. Otherwise we're just wasting our time on empty
externals.

Worse yet, those who enjoy the admiration of others
because of their outward "piety" have already received their
reward. Their "good deeds," done for show, have no merit in
God's eyes.

Christ tells us to practice our good deeds as quietly and
unobtrusively as possible—better yet, in secret, so that nobody
but God knows. Then there is no danger of mixed motives: a
desire for human respect and applause mixed in with a desire
to please God.

We have a natural human desire to be admired. But if we
persist in doing good quietly, that crass desire for praise will
gradually fade, to be replaced with a genuine desire to please
only God, regardless of what others may think or say.

MATTHEW 7:13–14

Enter by the narrow gate; for the gate is wide and the way is
easy, that leads to destruction, and those who enter by it are
many. For the gate is narrow and the way is hard, that leads
to life, and those who find it are few.

God, of course, wants everyone to be saved (see 1 Timothy 2:4),
but many people don't want what God wants. Sure, people say
they want to go to heaven, but many aren't willing to do what

is required, namely, to believe in the Lord, turn from sin and wholeheartedly obey him (see 1 John 3:21–24).

Christ certainly implies that, out of the vast number of human beings whom God will create, few will make it to heaven (see also Matthew 22:1–14; Luke 13:22–24). This is why the *Catechism of the Catholic Church* emphasizes the "urgent" nature of the call to conversion (see *CCC*, 1036).

Many of the great saints too, such as Saint Augustine, appeared to be rather pessimistic about people's prospects of entering eternal life.[4]

Read Christ's words again in the light of your own personal journey toward eternity. Ask yourself, "At this very moment, where am I headed? Am I on the broad and well-traveled road that leads to perdition, or am I truly striving to find and enter the narrow gate?"

ROMANS 3:27–31

Then what becomes of our boasting? It is excluded. On what principle? On the principle of works? No, but on the principle of faith. For we hold that a man is justified by faith apart from works of law. Or is God the God of Jews only? Is he not the God of Gentiles also? Yes, of Gentiles also, since God is one; and he will justify the circumcised on the ground of their faith and the uncircumcised through their faith. Do we then overthrow the law by this faith? By no means! On the contrary, we uphold the law.

Saint Paul was very careful to explain that salvation comes as a gift of God's grace. As he declares in this passage, we don't—in fact, we *can't*—earn it. We only receive it by grace through faith. So there is no room for boasting but only room for thanking God.

ROMANS 4:2—5

For if Abraham was justified by works, he has something to boast about, but not before God. For what does the Scripture say? "Abraham believed God, and it was reckoned to him as righteousness." Now to one who works, his wages are not reckoned as a gift but as his due. And to one who does not work but trusts him who justifies the ungodly, his faith is reckoned as righteousness.

Saint Paul reminds us that we are incapable of saving ourselves. We cooperate with God's saving grace through the "obedience of faith" (Romans 1:5; 16:26). Again, no boasting allowed.

ROMANS 5:12—14, 18—19

Therefore as sin came into the world through one man and death through sin, and so death spread to all men because all men sinned—sin indeed was in the world before the law was given, but sin is not counted where there is no law. Yet death reigned from Adam to Moses, even over those whose sins were not like the transgression of Adam, who was a type of the one who was to come.... Then as one man's trespass led to condemnation for all men, so one man's act of righteousness leads to acquittal and life for all men. For as by one man's disobedience many were made sinners, so by one man's obedience many will be made righteous.

If you ever encounter someone who denies the doctrine of original sin, share with him or her this summary of the fall of Adam and Eve. Their sin wounded all humanity and the whole cosmos.

But God did not leave us in that miserable state of alienation. He sent his only-begotten Son to heal the wound of sin.

Christ, the Second Adam, reversed the terrible tide of sin that had swept humanity away from God. Now, through Christ, we can come back to the Father as his sons and daughters, no longer living in exile.

ROMANS 6:1–4

What shall we say then? Are we to continue in sin that grace may abound? By no means! How can we who died to sin still live in it? Do you not know that all of us who have been baptized into Christ Jesus were baptized into his death? We were buried therefore with him by baptism into death, so that as Christ was raised from the dead by the glory of the Father, we too might walk in newness of life.

When Christ forgave the woman caught in adultery (see John 8:1–11), he told her to "go, and do not sin again." This is a very important lesson for all Christians to learn, for as Saint Paul says, once we have become members of the body of Christ, we should die to the flesh and avoid sin. This is what he means by walking in the newness of life. We are called to forsake our former ways of sin and walk in the light of God's grace.

Of course, this is easier said than done. But we must strive, by God's grace, to do it.

The next time you find yourself teetering on the brink of some sin, especially a serious one, recall this passage, and remember that you are a son or daughter of the light. Don't slink back into the darkness.

ROMANS 8:14–17

For all who are led by the Spirit of God are sons of God. For you did not receive the spirit of slavery to fall back into fear, but you have received the spirit of sonship. When we cry, "Abba!

Father!" it is the Spirit himself bearing witness with our spirit that we are children of God, and if children, then heirs, heirs of God and fellow heirs with Christ, provided we suffer with him in order that we may also be glorified with him.

Moses rescued the Hebrews from their crushing slavery in Egypt, and in so doing he acted as a prefigurement or "type" of Christ, who leads his people out of the slavery of sin. As Saint Paul reminds us, it is unthinkable that we should slide back into slavery. Every time we sin, especially when we sin mortally (see 1 John 5:16–17), we turn away from God, away from freedom, and head back into slavery. That is not how children and heirs of God should act!

ROMANS 11:22–23

Note then the kindness and the severity of God: severity toward those who have fallen, but God's kindness to you, provided you continue in his kindness; otherwise you too will be cut off. And even the others, if they do not persist in their unbelief, will be grafted in, for God has the power to graft them in again.

A Protestant minister once insisted to me that Catholics were "unbiblical" in their belief that Christians can lose their salvation. He was convinced that "once saved is always saved." So I quoted this passage from Saint Paul.

The minister was silent for a few seconds and then asked what version of Scripture I was using. It happened to be a Protestant translation. He opened his Bible to Romans 11 and read these words slowly to himself, almost as if for the first time. "I've never noticed that verse in this context before," he admitted.

Of course, he had *read* this passage innumerable times, but by his own admission, it had never "jumped out at him" the way it had just then. He simply had never really noticed in this light Saint Paul's warning here to his Christian audience (that is, the Romans) that they could lose their salvation if they do not remain in God's grace. Likening the Jews, God's chosen people, to a cultivated olive tree, Saint Paul says that some of them were like branches that were snapped off as a result of their rejection of their Messiah. These lost their salvation.

Saint Paul's clear teaching applies to all Christians, we moderns included. The question I asked that minister (which he really didn't have an answer to) was: "If Christians cannot lose their salvation, as you claim, then why would Saint Paul warn his audience about a danger that couldn't happen to them?"

GALATIANS 5:19–26

Now the works of the flesh are plain: immorality, impurity, licentiousness, idolatry, sorcery, enmity, strife, jealousy, anger, selfishness, dissension, party spirit, envy, drunkenness, carousing, and the like. I warn you, as I warned you before, that those who do such things shall not inherit the kingdom of God. But the fruit of the Spirit is love, joy, peace, patience, kindness, goodness, faithfulness, gentleness, self-control; against such there is no law. And those who belong to Christ Jesus have crucified the flesh with its passions and desires.

If we live by the Spirit, let us also walk by the Spirit. Let us have no self-conceit, no provoking of one another, no envy of one another.

This passage provides a veritable catalog of the sins of our age. The garish, scandal-mongering tabloids that assault the eye in the checkout line at the grocery store tell the tale. While mankind has a long history of wallowing in wicked behavior, this passage takes on a new level of urgency when we consider how very *public* these "works of the flesh" are today. Movies, television, popular music and the Internet purvey the seductive message that these behaviors are good.

Saint Paul warns that those who engage in such things "will not inherit the kingdom of God." To say it differently, unless they repent and turn back to Christ, they will wind up in hell for all eternity. The fact that he tells Christians, "I warn *you*," is yet another scriptural reminder that the "once saved, always saved" notion is just not true.

EPHESIANS 2:8–10

For by grace you have been saved through faith; and this is not your own doing, it is the gift of God—not because of works, lest any man should boast. For we are his workmanship, created in Christ Jesus for good works, which God prepared beforehand, that we should walk in them.

There are several things going on in this brief passage.

First, Saint Paul is driving home the fact, yet again, that we owe everything to God's gift of grace: our existence, our salvation, our faith, our ability to do good works—everything.[5]

Second, we receive this gift of grace through faith,[6] but notice what Saint Paul says: our faith is *itself* a gift of God. Notice, though, that God does not have faith in himself *for* us. He enables us with his grace to have faith in him, but it is we who must have the faith. In other words, our faith is a *work*—a conscious act of the will—that we have been enabled by God's grace to carry out to his glory.

Third, our own works cannot save us—if they could, there would have been no need for the Incarnation and the atoning death of Christ on the cross. But we are, as Saint Paul points out, created by God to walk in good works. With his grace he enables the justified man or woman to do good works that are meritorious and pleasing to him. As Saint Augustine said, "What, therefore, is the merit of man before grace by which merit he should receive grace? Since only grace makes every good merit of ours, and when God crowns our merits, *he crowns nothing else but His own gifts*."[7]

PHILIPPIANS 2:12–13

Therefore, my beloved, as you have always obeyed, so now, not only as in my presence but much more in my absence, work out your own salvation with fear and trembling; for God is at work in you, both to will and to work for his good pleasure.

Scripture tells us to "work out our salvation with fear and trembling," not because we should be afraid that God will not keep his word but because we are entirely capable of not keeping ours (see 2 Timothy 2:13). We should fear our own weakness but love and trust God with all our hearts.

The beloved and holy priest Saint John Vianney (known as the Curé of Ars) composed this little prayer, which may help you focus better on loving and trusting God each day: "I love you, O my God, and my only desire is to love you until the last breath of my life. I love you, O my infinitely lovable God, and I would rather die loving you, than live without loving you. I love you, Lord, and the only grace I ask is to love you eternally...My God, if my tongue cannot say in every moment that I love you, I want my heart to repeat it to you as often as I draw breath" (*CCC*, 2658).

HEBREWS 10:26—29

If we sin deliberately after receiving the knowledge of the truth, there no longer remains a sacrifice for sins, but a fearful prospect of judgment, and a fury of fire which will consume the adversaries. A man who has violated the law of Moses dies without mercy at the testimony of two or three witnesses. How much worse punishment do you think will be deserved by the man who has spurned the Son of God, and profaned the blood of the covenant by which he was sanctified, and outraged the Spirit of grace?

Here is another helpful passage to share with those who claim that the Bible teaches an absolute "eternal security" for Christians. Notice that the writer says, "If *we* sin deliberately." The only people who had "received the knowledge of the truth" and thereby been "sanctified by the covenant blood" were Christians. So it is clear to whom this warning applies.

The Christian who turns away from God and returns to a life of sin suffers worse punishment than the person who never was sanctified by the "covenant blood" of Christ.

JAMES 2:14—17, 20—26

What does it profit, my brethren, if a man says he has faith but has not works? Can his faith save him? If a brother or sister is poorly clothed and in lack of daily food, and one of you says to them, "Go in peace, be warmed and filled," without giving them the things needed for the body, what does it profit? So faith by itself, if it has no works, is dead....

Do you want to be shown, you foolish fellow [that is, you ignoramus], that faith apart from works is barren? Was not Abraham our father justified by works, when he offered his son Isaac upon the altar? You see that faith was active along with his works, and faith was completed by works, and the Scripture was fulfilled which says, "Abraham believed God, and it was reckoned to him as righteousness"; and he was called the friend of God. You see that a man is justified by works and not by faith alone. And in the same way was not also Rahab the harlot justified by works when she received the messengers and sent them out another way? For as the body apart from the spirit is dead, so faith apart from works is dead.

Several years ago I participated in a spirited public debate with three Protestant ministers on the subject of the Protestant theory of justification by faith alone (Latin: *sola fide*).[8] What made the debate particularly interesting, not to mention sad, was to watch the contortions and gyrations these ministers went though in their attempt to deny the plain meaning of this biblical text, the heart of which is, *"You see that a man is justified by works and not by faith alone."* This clear biblical teaching stands in direct contrast with the "tradition of men" (see Mathtew 15:6–9) that arose at the time of the Protestant Reformation, known as *sola fide*, which claims that human beings are justified only *"extrinsically"* or *"forensically,"* meaning that God declares the sinner righteous solely on the merits of the One who is truly righteous, Jesus Christ. But according to this view, the sinner is not really made righteous, he's just declared righteous.

Volumes of learned discourse have been written about this vexing, long-standing disagreement between the Catholic Church, representing historic Christianity, and the various Protestant denominations who glommed on to this notion of *sola fide* in the wake of Martin Luther's revolt against the Catholic Church. It would be simply impossible to do any kind of justice (pardon the pun) to this topic in only a few meager paragraphs, but we can at least take note here of the fact that the Bible is clear in James 2, as well as in passages such as

Matthew 7:21–26; 19:16–22; 25:31–41; Romans 2:2–10; Galatians 5:6; Philippians 2:12–13; Ephesians 2:8–9; 1 John 3:21; 5:2; Revelation 2:2–23 and so on, that after our initial justification,[9] our good works, done in and by the grace of God, do contribute to our justification and growth in holiness (see *CCC*, 162, 1446–1447, 2001–2016).

1 JOHN 3:19—24

By this we shall know that we are of the truth, and reassure our hearts before him whenever our hearts condemn us; for God is greater than our hearts, and he knows everything. Beloved, if our hearts do not condemn us, we have confidence before God; and we receive from him whatever we ask, because we keep his commandments and do what pleases him. And this is his commandment, that we should believe in the name of his Son Jesus Christ and love one another, just as he has commanded us. All who keep his commandments abide in him, and he in them. And by this we know that he abides in us, by the Spirit which he has given us.

Here we see the twofold nature of the Christian life: faith and works. As the old song says, "You can't have one without the other." If you believe in Jesus Christ but do not live out that faith through obedience to his commandments, you have an empty, lifeless faith that cannot save you.

Conversely, if you are loaded with "good works" but do not have true faith in Christ, you are also fooling yourself. You cannot obligate God to let you into heaven by "doing stuff."

Saint John here points out what Christ wants: faith *and* works or, as Saint Paul calls it in Galatians 5:6, "*faith working through love.*" Accept no substitutions.

1 JOHN 5:13–17

I write this to you who believe in the name of the Son of God, that you may know that you have eternal life. And this is the confidence which we have in him, that if we ask anything according to his will he hears us. And if we know that he hears us in whatever we ask, we know that we have obtained the requests made of him. If any one sees his brother committing what is not a deadly sin, he will ask, and God will give him life for those whose sin is not deadly. There is sin which is deadly; I do not say that one is to pray for that. All wrongdoing is sin, but there is sin which is not deadly.

We read here about our blessed assurance of salvation in Jesus Christ (see Colossians 2:2; Hebrews 6:11; 10:22; 11:1). We should have confidence in this promise, knowing that God will never change his mind or revoke his promise.

But an often overlooked truth immediately follows: We ourselves can revoke our acceptance of God's promise of eternal life by rebelling against him through a degree of sin that the Bible here calls "deadly" (also translated "mortal"). This is an important scriptural foundation for the Catholic Church's teaching on the reality of mortal sin (see *CCC*, 1854–1864).

CHAPTER 4
Divine Revelation

DEUTERONOMY 30:11—14

> For this commandment which I command you this day is not too hard for you, neither is it far off. It is not in heaven, that you should say, "Who will go up for us to heaven, and bring it to us, that we may hear it and do it?" Neither is it beyond the sea, that you should say, "Who will go over the sea for us, and bring it to us, that we may hear it and do it?" But the word is very near you; it is in your mouth and in your heart, so that you can do it.

Sometimes God seems to ask too much of us. Often what's really going on is that we are reacting selfishly to his will. What he wants is not too hard; rather, deep down inside, we are lazy and complacent. Sound familiar?

In this passage God reminds us that we don't have to be superhuman to live according to his plan: We just have to be *willing*. Yet as we all know from experience in the spiritual life, just being willing to put aside our selfish little projects and do what God wants can be very hard.

The Lord is reminding us here that we don't have to do the impossible. We only have to take a deep breath, trust in him and say, "Yes, Lord." He will supply all the grace, strength and courage we need to see it through. Try it. You'll see.

ISAIAH 1:18—19

Come now, let us reason together,
  says the LORD:
though your sins are like scarlet,
  they shall be as white as snow;

> though they are red like crimson,
>> they shall become like wool.
> If you are willing and obedient,
>> you shall eat the good of the land.

God created human beings in his own image (see Genesis 1:26–27), which means that, like God, we have an intellect and a will.[1] He wants us to use that gift of reason in our efforts to know the world around us and our place in it.

Some people imagine that faith is somehow contrary to reason, but this is not the case. True faith is based on reason—one of God's highest gifts to us—and has nothing to fear from the truths we can ascertain from the use of our reason. But of course, human reason can only carry us so far, and sometimes that's not very far at all. Which is why the Lord supplies what we lack in the form of divine revelation, namely Sacred Scripture and Sacred Tradition.

In Scripture God reveals his loving plan of salvation through Jesus Christ. This plan begins with his desire to cleanse us from all our iniquities. He wants to purify us and heal us of our many self-inflicted wounds of sin.

God will not force us to accept this great gift. He invites us to accept it, and he even is willing to reason with us through his two "books" of natural and supernatural revelation, the material universe (see Psalm 19:1–4; Romans 1:18–21) and Sacred Scripture. But in the end he loves us too much to trample on our freedom. Those who accept his free gift of grace (see Ephesians 2:8–9) and become "willing and obedient" to his will experience the life-giving transformation from sin to grace, from death to life.

MATTHEW 7:15–20

Beware of false prophets, who come to you in sheep's clothing but inwardly are ravenous wolves. You will know them by their fruits. Are grapes gathered from thorns, or figs from thistles?

So, every sound tree bears good fruit, but the bad tree bears evil fruit. A sound tree cannot bear evil fruit, nor can a bad tree bear good fruit. Every tree that does not bear good fruit is cut down and thrown into the fire. Thus you will know them by their fruits.

There are many false prophets out there: Smiling faces, soothing voices and seemingly true ideologies beckon us from all sides. But Jesus warned that behind some pleasant and attractive exteriors lie deception and error. He has given us tools to help us distinguish between friend and foe, between truth and error.

Foremost among these is divine revelation, found in the preaching and teaching of the Apostles and preserved for us in a unique way in Sacred Tradition and, par excellence, in Sacred Scripture. We have the Catholic Church, established by Jesus Christ as a sure guide to the truth (see Matthew 16:18–19, 18:18, 28:18–20; Luke 10:16). And of course, we have the gift of our intellect, which God illuminates with the light of his truth.

Pope John Paul II wrote:

> The splendor of truth shines forth in the works of the Creator and, in a special way, in man, created in the image and likeness of God (cf. Gen 1:26). Truth enlightens man's intelligence and shapes his freedom, leading him to know and love the Lord. Hence the Psalmist prays: "Let the light of your face shine on us, O Lord" (Ps 4:6)....
>
> Called to salvation through faith in Jesus Christ, "the true light that enlightens everyone" (Jn 1:9), people become "light in the Lord" and "children of light" (Eph 5:8), and are made holy by "obedience to the truth" (1 Pet 1:22).[2]

So check any message you encounter to see if it is consistent with the teachings of Scripture and the Church. If it isn't, cast it aside (see 1 Thessalonians 5:21). If you stay close to the Lord through prayer and the sacraments, remain attentive to his commandments and always seek to be in communion with the Church,[3] you will have no need to be concerned with false prophets and their false messages.

ACTS 17:10—11

The brethren immediately sent Paul and Silas away by night to Beroea; and when they arrived they went into the Jewish synagogue. Now these Jews were more noble than those in Thessalonica, for they received the word with all eagerness, examining the scriptures daily to see if these things were so.

This verse is often raised as a proof text in favor of the Protestant theory of *sola scriptura*, but it is hardly evidence that the Apostles taught the notion of the formal sufficiency of Scripture.[4] Yes, Saint Luke called the Berean Jews "more noble" because they examined the Jewish Scriptures to see if what Paul had been preaching to them could be reconciled with the written Word of God. They certainly were more noble specifically because they didn't *riot* violently against Paul and Silas, as did the Thessalonian Jews, who would have none of it when Paul preached Christ to them. But for the following reasons, this doesn't somehow prove that Scripture is sufficient.

First, these were Jews, so it only makes sense that Paul would appeal to their Scripture in his defense of Christ. Of course they would check the sacred texts to see if these things were true—mainly because Paul challenged them to do so.

Second, when preaching to pagan audiences (see Acts 17:16–34), Paul did not appeal to Scripture, since the pagans had no regard for it as the Jews did. Paul met them at a level they could understand.

And finally, there were Jews who read Scripture and interpreted it wrongly—a danger that is still present today—which is why they needed Paul and the other apostolic members of the original Magisterium to interpret it for them.

ROMANS 2:12—16

All who have sinned without the law will also perish without the law, and all who have sinned under the law will be judged by the law. For it is not the hearers of the law who are righteous before God, but the doers of the law who will be justified. When Gentiles who have not the law do by nature what the law requires, they are a law to themselves, even though they do not have the law. They show that what the law requires is written on their hearts, while their conscience also bears witness and their conflicting thoughts accuse or perhaps excuse them on that day when, according to my gospel, God judges the secrets of men by Christ Jesus.

Everyone everywhere knows that certain things are just plain wrong: murder, theft and lying are three examples. There seems to exist a universal instinct that certain actions should be avoided. This is a kind of real-world proof of what Saint Paul is saying here. God's law is inscribed on the human heart, even when someone tries to block it out.

I CORINTHIANS 15:1—3

Now I would remind you, brethren, in what terms I preached to you the gospel, which you received, in which you stand, by which you are saved, if you hold it fast—unless you believed in vain.

For I delivered to you as of first importance what I also received, that Christ died for our sins in accordance with the Scriptures.

This passage is another instance where Saint Paul explains the importance of Sacred Tradition. He refers us to the body of teaching that he received—both from the Risen Christ, after his conversion, and under the inspiration of the Holy Spirit (see 1 Thessalonians 2:13)—and that he handed on to the Church.

This motif of *receiving* and *handing on* is the essence of the Catholic teaching on what Tradition is and what it does.[5]

Notice also that Paul emphasizes that what he received and handed on is "in accordance with the Scriptures." In other words, Tradition and Scripture are two mutually complementary modes of handing on the faith (see Luke 1:1–4; 2 Thessalonians 2:15) that was "once for all" given to the Church (Jude 3).

1 THESSALONIANS 2:13

And we also thank God constantly for this, that when you received the word of God which you heard from us, you accepted it not as the word of men but as what it really is, the word of God, which is at work in you believers.

Saint Paul identifies apostolic *preaching* as being fully the word of God. Saint Basil of Caesarea declared: "Of the beliefs and practices whether generally accepted or enjoined which are preserved in the Church, some we possess derived from written teaching; others we have delivered to us 'in a mystery' by the tradition of the apostles; and *both of these in relation to true religion have the same force*."[6]

2 THESSALONIANS 2:15

So then, brethren, stand firm and hold to the traditions which you were taught by us, either by word of mouth or by letter.

God's revelation to his people in the New Testament era came first through oral preaching and teaching (see Luke 1:1–4). Only later, and in some cases much later, did the apostolic authors begin to set down in writing some of that teaching for the purpose of dealing with particular problems in the early

Church, as well as for making their teaching "portable," that is, able to be disseminated throughout all the places where the Church had begun to grow and which the Apostles were not able to visit in person. After the Apostles died, the New Testament Scriptures rose to a supreme level of prominence and importance in the Church, since they represented the teachings of the Apostles and were thus a precious heritage of divinely inspired truth for all future generations.

But Scripture does not function in a vacuum. It requires a human interpreter, either the individual Christian or the teaching office of the Church as a whole (that is, the Magisterium). And so this teaching of Saint Paul is important to remember: God teaches his people through both Scripture and Tradition.

We see Tradition enshrined in the Church's liturgy, her sacraments and her prayers, and these help us remain faithful to the authentic *meaning* of the sacred text. Without these the Lord would have left his people in the hopeless predicament of "every man for himself" when it comes to interpreting the Bible. Christ placed Scripture within the context of the Church, to be preached and meditated on, studied, proclaimed and prayed over with the guidance he promised (see Luke 10:16). Thus we know that the Church's understanding of these Scriptures conforms to their authentic meaning.

2 TIMOTHY 3:16–17

All Scripture is inspired by God and profitable for teaching, for reproof, for correction, and for training in righteousness, that the man of God may be complete, equipped for every good work.

Saint John Chrysostom (347–407), the great Catholic preacher and Scripture scholar who was the archbishop of Constantinople, spoke about the importance of Scripture "for teaching, for reproof, for correction, and for training in righteousness." If you follow his wise advice, you will truly become a man or woman of God who will be "complete" and "equipped for every good work":

> I am always encouraging you to pay attention not only to what is said here in church, but also, when you are at home, to continue constantly in the practice of reading the divine Scriptures.... For let not anyone say to me those silly words,...." Reading the Bible isn't my thing. That's for those...who have a way of life without interruptions."
>
> What are you saying, man? It's not your business to pay attention to the Bible because you are distracted by thousands of concerns? Then Bible reading belongs more to you than to the monks! For they do not make as much use of the help of the divine Scriptures as those who always have a great many things to do.... But you are always standing in the line of battle and are constantly being hit, so you need more medicine. For not only does your spouse irritate you, but your son annoys you,...an enemy schemes against you, a colleague trips you up.... Numerous powerful inducements to anger and anxiety, to discouragement and grief, to vanity and loss of sense surround us on every side....
>
> Since many things of this kind besiege our soul, we need the divine medicines, so that we might treat the wounds we already have, and so that we might check beforehand the wounds that are not yet, but are going to be,...for it is...not possible for anyone to be saved who does not constantly have the benefit of spiritual reading.[7]

2 PETER 1:20–21; 3:15–16

First of all you must understand this, that no prophecy of Scripture is a matter of one's own interpretation, because no prophecy ever came by the impulse of man, but men moved by the Holy Spirit spoke from God....

> And count the forbearance of our Lord as salvation. So also
> our beloved brother Paul wrote to you according to the wis-
> dom given him, speaking of this as he does in all his letters.
> There are some things in them hard to understand, which
> the ignorant and unstable twist to their own destruction, as
> they do the other Scriptures.

Chances are, as you've channel-surfed television or radio, you've run across preachers loudly proclaiming that "the Bible teaches *this*!" or "the Bible teaches *that*!" to promote some out-landish and patently untrue opinion. This has been happening for a very long time; indeed, since the time of the Apostles there have been many who misunderstand and misuse Sacred Scripture. The Arians of the fourth and fifth centuries, for example, did exactly this in their denial of the Trinity and their quest to prove that Jesus Christ is not God.[8]

Erroneous interpretations of Scripture abound in today's splintered Christian world. There are sincere people who are sincerely wrong in some of the interpretations they impose on Scripture. Then there are those who "twist" Scripture's mean-ing. This passage says that they do so "to their own *destruc-tion*"—very strong language, to say the least.

The Catholic Church has the answer to this long-standing problem. It's called "Sacred Tradition," which is the Church's lived understanding of the *meaning* of Scripture, including statements such as "My flesh is food indeed, and my blood is drink indeed; he who eats my flesh and drinks my blood abides in me, and I in him" (John 6:55–56), and "If you forgive the sins of any, they are forgiven; if you retain the sins of any, they are retained" (John 20:23).[9]

We always should be careful to check our understanding of Sacred Scripture to make sure it is in conformity with the 2,000-year Tradition of the Catholic Church. For Christ entrusted the Church with the duty of faithfully proclaiming to each generation the authentic meaning of the "faith which was once for all delivered to the saints" (Jude 3; see Matthew 28:18–20; Luke 10:16).

REVELATION 22:18–19

I warn every one who hears the words of the prophecy of this book: if any one adds to them, God will add to him the plagues described in this book, and if any one takes away from the words of the book of this prophecy, God will take away his share in the tree of life and in the holy city, which are described in this book.

When taken in isolation, this passage might appear to corroborate the *sola scriptura* position. However, when we look at the context of the passage and the wider framework of the scriptural message, it becomes clear that the phrase "this book" refers to the Book of Revelation, not to the Bible as a whole.

When Saint John wrote Revelation, the Bible as we know it today (that is, seventy-three books of inspired Scripture compiled into a single volume) did not exist. It was the Catholic Church that would eventually gather and codify the various New Testament writings into the Bible as we have it today.[10]

John's warning was to those who might try to import additional (and very likely erroneous) ideas into his work or to remove things from it. This was a widespread problem in the first several centuries of Christianity—one the Apostle was well aware of, hence his stern warning to the reader.

In Deuteronomy 4 Moses said very much the same thing that John did: "You shall not add to the word which I command you, nor take from it" (Deuteronomy 4:2). No one today would argue that nothing beyond Deuteronomy should have been added to Scripture. Neither can we argue that the Revelation passage shows the Bible alone to be sufficient.

CHAPTER 5
The Church

ISAIAH 9:6—7

For to us a child is born,
    to us a son is given;
and the government will be upon his shoulder,
    and his name will be called
"Wonderful Counselor, Mighty God,
    Everlasting Father, Prince of Peace."
Of the increase of his government and of peace
    there will be no end,
upon the throne of David, and over his kingdom,
    to establish it, and to uphold it
with justice and with righteousness
    from this time forth and for evermore.

This prophetic passage refers to Christ and his kingdom, and there are many things that can be said about the mighty truths contained in it. But let's focus here on an often unnoticed aspect: the *permanence* of Christ's kingdom.

"There will be no end," Isaiah tells us, to Christ's rule. This is a helpful fact to remember in apologetic discussions with Mormons, for instance. They believe that there was a total apostasy of the Church Christ had founded by about the middle of the third century, and that for the ensuing fifteen centuries, the true Church did not exist on earth.[1]

Isaiah's prophecy assures us that Mormonism's "total apostasy" theory cannot be true. The Church Christ established is "without end" and "for evermore." This is the Catholic Church, which has withstood the vagaries of time.

MATTHEW 28:18—20

Jesus came and said to them, "All authority in heaven and on earth has been given to me. Go therefore and make disciples of all nations, baptizing them in the name of the Father and of the Son and of the Holy Spirit, teaching them to observe all that I have commanded you; and behold, I am with you always, to the close of the age."

This passage is known as the "Great Commission." Here we see the Lord, shortly before his ascension into heaven, sending his Apostles, with his own authority, to conquer the world for the truth. Notice that this commission (that is, *sending forth*) involves several important elements.

First, these chosen men are sent into the *whole* world. In other words, this Church that the Lord has established is for all people at all times and in all places. In other words, it is *universal*. "Universal," in fact, is the root meaning of the word *catholic*.

Second, these men are sent with the singular mission of making *converts* (disciples), not merely "fellow travelers" or like-minded partisans who may or may not agree in some vague and general way with their teachings. The call of Christ to these first Apostles was clear and specific and decisive: Invite everyone, always and everywhere, to pass through the doorway of conversion into his Church. This is normatively accomplished through the sacrament of baptism.

Third, the Apostles were preaching the Good News of Jesus Christ, who was now teaching the world *through* the Church he had established on the rock of Peter. These teachings were faithfully and clearly delivered to the original generations of Christians, initially through oral tradition—that is, apostolic preaching (see 1 Thessalonians 2:13)—and, beginning years later, through the New Testament. Note that these teachings came not from the Apostles but from Christ, who instructed them, and from the Holy Spirit, who led them into all truth (see John 14:25–26; 16:13).

Fourth, notice that Christ promised that he would be with his Church *forever*—until "the close of the age." Since he is God and can neither deceive us nor be deceived by us, we can count on this promise. This unfolds into the truth that there cannot be a time when Christ's Church would cease to exist.

And this scriptural truth serves us in another significant way: The only Church that the facts of history show to have existed in an unbroken line of continuity, from the time Christ uttered these words to our present day, is the Catholic Church. No other Christian group, denomination or fellowship can come anywhere close to credibly making that claim and backing it up with solid historical evidence. Again, only the Catholic Church can do that.

MARK 4:36–41

And leaving the crowd, they took [Jesus] with them, just as he was, in the boat. And other boats were with him. And a great storm of wind arose, and the waves beat into the boat, so that the boat was already filling. But he was in the stern, asleep on the cushion; and they woke him and said to him, "Teacher, do you not care if we perish?" And he awoke and rebuked the wind, and said to the sea, "Peace! Be still!" And the wind ceased, and there was a great calm. He said to them, "Why are you afraid? Have you no faith?" And they were filled with awe, and said to one another, "Who then is this, that even wind and sea obey him?"

Over the past twenty years, I've spent a *lot* of time on airplanes, crisscrossing not only North America but the world, often logging over a 100,000 miles a year in order to speak about the Catholic Faith at universities, parishes and conferences. One thing I've learned for sure: When there's turbulence during a flight, I keep an eye on the flight attendants. If they don't seem to be bothered by it, then I'm not bothered. But when I see flight attendants get nervous, that's when I get nervous. After all, these folks are familiar with just about anything nature can throw at a plane.

Similarly, several of the Apostles made their living as fishermen on the Sea of Galilee. Their panic in this passage shows that these were serious winds and waves, not an ordinary storm. And Christ was asleep.

Can you imagine their frantic efforts to wake Jesus, not to mention a possible sense of irritation at his being asleep during this life-threatening ordeal? "Teacher," they demanded of him, "do you not *care* if we perish?"

Whoa! I find these words so unpleasantly relevant to our own day that they practically make my hair stand on end. The Catholic Church is being buffeted by immense waves of scandal, apathy, corruption and hostility, a good deal of it—such as the recent priest sexual scandals—from within the Church. God, help us!

And yet, we see a glimmer of hope in this Scripture passage. For no sooner did the disciples awaken Jesus than he acted to calm the storm. *Whoa!* This man had the power to command the forces of wind and rain. Can you imagine the slack-jawed amazement of the disciples as they watched him operate?

The truth is that, although Jesus was asleep, not for a moment had he forgotten those he loved. The danger the Apostles faced that day was only apparent, not lethal. And so it is today. Christ is present in his Church just as much as he was in the boat that very tumultuous afternoon on the Sea of Galilee. And he will not allow his Church to sink beneath the stormy waves of dissent, priest scandals, sinful laity, the hostility of the world or anything else that may threaten its survival.

LUKE 10:16

He who hears you hears me, and he who rejects you rejects me, and he who rejects me rejects him who sent me.

This is one of those important passages in Scripture that deserve a great deal of paper and ink and contemplation to properly comprehend. However, since space in this lowly book is limited, we must be content to focus on one key aspect: Jesus Christ established a Church and appointed certain men in it to speak for him, with his authority, after he ascended into heaven (see Matthew 28:19–20).

Christ's words, "He who hears you hears me," signify both a promise of his continual presence in the teaching Church and his presence in the hearts and minds of those who believe on account of the testimony of that Church. They also entail at least the implication of the Church's teaching of infallibility, because if the Apostles—and by extension their successors, that is, the bishops of the Church who form its Magisterium—were to formally teach error, then Christ would have put himself in an impossible situation with only two outcomes.

One option would be that the Apostles were able to formally teach error, but then God would have to ratify that error. That, of course, would be impossible, for God can neither deceive nor be deceived.

The other possibility would be that Christ was either ignorant or lying when he made this promise. But then he could not be God, who is all-knowing and who is the Truth. We can rule out that possibility, as well.

This promise of authority carries momentous implications for the Church. Christ sent the Apostles into the world with his authority, and through apostolic succession, their successors inherit this protection from formally teaching error (see CCC, 889).[2]

JOHN 14:25–26

These things I have spoken to you, while I am still with you. But the Counselor, the Holy Spirit, whom the Father will send in my name, he will teach you all things, and bring to your remembrance all that I have said to you.

The Lord, knowing that he would soon be ascending to the Father, did not intend to leave the infant Church without his guiding presence. His promise that he and the Father would send the Holy Spirit was proof of this. From the Day of Pentecost onward, the Holy Spirit has continued to guide, illuminate and invigorate the Church, and his presence with us is yet another indication of the authentic teaching mission of the Catholic Church.

ACTS 9:1–5

But Saul, still breathing threats and murder against the disciples of the Lord, went to the high priest and asked him for letters to the synagogues at Damascus, so that if he found any belonging to the Way, men or women, he might bring them bound to Jerusalem. Now as he journeyed he approached Damascus, and suddenly a light from heaven flashed about him. And he fell to the ground and heard a voice saying to him, "Saul, Saul, why do you persecute me?" And he said, "Who are you, Lord?" And he said, "I am Jesus, whom you are persecuting."

Conversions don't get any more dramatic than this! Not only did the Lord bring this man Saul, who was a deadly foe of the Catholic Church, to repentance and conversion, but he also revealed in this exchange a deep truth about the Church.

Notice that when Saul asked who was speaking to him, the response was, "I am Jesus, *whom you are persecuting.*" Now, Saul had never met Christ in person, and the people he was persecuting were Christians. But the Lord tells him, "You are persecuting *me.*" This shows us that Christians are quite literally members of the body of Christ (see 1 Corinthians 12:12–27), not in some kind of nebulous, figurative way but really and truly.

ROMANS 10:9–15

If you confess with your lips that Jesus is Lord and believe in your heart that God raised him from the dead, you will be saved. For man believes with his heart and so is justified, and he confesses with his lips and so is saved. The Scripture says, "No one who believes in him will be put to shame." For there is no distinction between Jew and Greek; the same Lord is Lord of all and bestows his riches upon all who call upon him. For, "every one who calls upon the name of the Lord will be saved."

But how are men to call upon him in whom they have not believed? And how are they to believe in him of whom they have never heard? And how are they to hear without a preacher? And how can men preach unless they are sent?

Notice how this passage emphasizes the *proclaimed* nature of faith in Christ. It presents a very human, incarnational dimension of faith. If you "confess with your lips," Saint Paul says, you will be saved. There is something so very human (that is, flesh and blood) about this.

Which makes perfect sense when we consider that the Second Person of the Trinity became not an angel (pure spirit) nor an animal (a material being with no rational soul) but a *man*—the one being who is a composite of spirit and matter. So when Saint Paul tells us that our faith in Christ depends first on "hearing" his message, then "calling upon" him in repentance and conversion and finally "confessing" our faith in him, we see how lovingly God has deigned to reach out to us. He speaks to us in a language that he has enabled us to understand and with which we can reply.

There is another very important message in this passage. Saint Paul explains that Christ entrusted the message to his chosen Apostles, those whom he commissioned and sent forth with the word of truth on their lips (see Matthew 28:19–20). In other words, we come to true faith in Christ through the medium of those whom he sent to teach us.

This poses no barrier between us and God. Rather, it is a bridge over which God comes directly to us. This is part of the mystery of the establishment of the Catholic Church. The Lord chose and set apart and then sent forth men to whom he had given his own authority to preach and teach in his name. This is yet another reminder of why it is so important that we listen to the Church Christ established, keeping clearly in mind his statement that dovetails so well with these words of Paul in Romans: "He who hears you hears me; and he who rejects you rejects me" (Luke 10:16).

1 CORINTHIANS 1:10

I appeal to you, brethren, by the name of our Lord Jesus Christ, that all of you agree and that there be no dissensions among you, but that you be united in the same mind and the same judgment. (See Romans 16:17–18.)

Unity is one of the four marks of the Catholic Church. The *Catechism* explains this principle and why it is so vital:

The Church is one because of her source: "the highest exemplar and source of this mystery is the unity, in the Trinity of Persons, of one God, the Father and the Son in the Holy Spirit" [Vatican II, *Unitatis Redintegratio*, 2 § 5].

The Church is one *because of her founder*: for "the Word made flesh, the prince of peace, reconciled all men to God by the cross, . . . restoring the unity of all in one people and one body" [*Gaudium et Spes*, 78 § 3]. The Church is one *because of her "soul"*: "It is the Holy Spirit, dwelling in those who believe and pervading and ruling over the entire Church, who brings about that wonderful communion of the faithful and joins them together so intimately in Christ that he is the principle of the Church's unity [*Unitatis Redintegratio*, 2 § 2]." Unity is of the essence of the Church:

> What an astonishing mystery! There is one Father of the universe, one Logos of the universe, and also one Holy Spirit, everywhere one and the same. There is also one virgin become mother, and I should like to call her "Church." [Saint Clement of Alexandria, *Paed.* 1, 6, 42; PG 8, 300]

From the beginning this one Church has been marked by a great *diversity* which comes from both the variety of God's gifts and the diversity of those who receive them. Within the unity of the People of God, a multiplicity of peoples and cultures is gathered together. Among the Church's members, there are different gifts, offices, conditions and ways of life. "Holding a rightful place in the communion of the Church there are also particular Churches that retain their own traditions" [*Lumen Gentium*, 13 § 2]. The great richness of such diversity is not opposed to the Church's unity. Yet sin and the burden of its consequences constantly threaten the gift of unity. And so the Apostle has to exhort Christians to "maintain the unity of the Spirit in the bond of peace" [Eph 4:3]. (CCC, 813–814)[3]

As Saint Paul explains in 1 Corinthians 1:10, the Lord desires unity based on truth, not compromise.

GALATIANS 1:6–9

I am astonished that you are so quickly deserting him who called you in the grace of Christ and turning to a different gospel—not that there is another gospel, but there are some who trouble you and want to pervert the gospel of Christ. But even if we, or an angel from heaven, should preach to you a gospel contrary to that which we preached to you, let him be accursed. As we have said before, so now I say again, If any one is preaching to you a gospel contrary to that which you received, let him be accursed.

It's one of those strange but appropriate coincidences that, in the Cathedral of the Madeline in Salt Lake City, Utah, this passage is emblazoned beneath a stern statue of Saint Paul, whose hand is gesturing vaguely in the direction of the Mormon Temple just a few miles away. Atop that temple is a gilded statue of the Book of Mormon personage Moroni, the "angel" who allegedly preached a very "different gospel" to Joseph Smith, who launched the Mormon Church in 1831.

Saint Paul tells us twice in this passage to reject any preaching that is incompatible with the true gospel of Jesus Christ. So the next time some well-intentioned but misguided missionaries show up on your doorstep with a satchel full of literature about their "gospel," you can politely quote Galatians 1:6–9, assure them of your prayers and send them on their way. For, as a Catholic, you already are in the one true Church established by Christ. Never forget that.

And do pray for those sincere but seriously misguided Mormon missionaries, that they too might discover the *true* gospel of Jesus Christ in the Catholic Church and embrace it.

HEBREWS 13:7—9

Remember your leaders, those who spoke to you the word of God; consider the outcome of their life, and imitate their faith. Jesus Christ is the same yesterday and today and forever. Do not be led away by diverse and strange teachings.

The truth of the gospel of Jesus Christ doesn't change. It isn't subject to historical "conditioning." It can't be "customized" to fit every taste and whim.

Since Christ is the same yesterday, today and forever, his teachings are likewise eternally true and immutable. Therefore we should follow the example of his saints, the countless heroic men and women who lived in joyful conformity to the truth, regardless of how others tried to dissuade them—even if their fidelity to Christ cost them their lives.

While we pray constantly to the Lord for grace and guidance, we can embrace with confidence the truths the Catholic Church teaches. Remember that Christ established his Church to *teach* us all those things he commands us to do (see Matthew 28:19-20). He promised that whoever listens to his Church is listening to him, and he warned that whoever rejects his Church's voice is rejecting him (see Luke 10:16).

CHAPTER 6
Evangelization

ISAIAH 6:5–8

And I said: "Woe is me! For I am lost; for I am a man of unclean lips, and I dwell in the midst of a people of unclean lips; for my eyes have seen the King, the LORD of hosts!"

Then flew one of the seraphim to me, having in his hand a burning coal which he had taken with tongs from the altar. And he touched my mouth, and said: "Behold, this has touched your lips; your guilt is taken away, and your sin forgiven." And I heard the voice of the Lord saying, "Whom shall I send, and who will go for us?" Then I said, "Here am I! Send me."

One doesn't have to look far for evidence that we live in the midst of an "unclean" society. Television, movies, the Internet and the media in general have swamped society with immorality, godlessness and a growing hostility toward Christianity. In the face of all these challenges, this Scripture passage holds out hope to us.

Notice that God cleansed Isaiah of his sins and then sent him back to his people as a prophet. How might this apply to you?

We all stand in need of God's purifying grace. And he desires that each of us be willing to speak as well as live the truth, as witnesses to those around us (see Matthew 5:14–16; 1 Peter 3:15). Ask him to touch the burning coal of his truth to *your* mouth, so that you will become ready and willing to say, "Here I am, Lord. Send me."

MATTHEW 10:16—20

Behold, I send you out as sheep in the midst of wolves; so be wise as serpents and innocent as doves. Beware of men; for they will deliver you up to councils, and flog you in their synagogues, and you will be dragged before governors and kings for my sake, to bear testimony before them and the Gentiles. When they deliver you up, do not be anxious about how you are to speak or what you are to say; for what you are to say will be given to you in that hour; for it is not you who speak, but the Spirit of your Father speaking through you.

You can't blame someone for feeling a slight shiver of dread when reading these grim words. The very idea of being dragged before some smug government official, tortured and perhaps even put to death is frightening. But look beyond the fearful scenario and see the deeper meaning Christ is revealing to us here.

Beginning with the Apostles and disciples, the Lord consoles and strengthens all who are willing to witness to others about him. Saint Stephen, a deacon and the first martyr of the Church, spoke God's word bravely and received a wondrous vision of the Lord just before he was stoned to death (Acts 7:8–60). Countless men, women and children have followed in his courageous footsteps.

Take courage in stories of these Christians, ordinary people like you and I, who were called to speak before governors and kings about their faith in Christ. Most likely we will never face anything so dramatic. But we too, each in our own way, will have our moments to stand up and speak about Jesus. Let's remember to rely not on our own cleverness but on God's grace. If we trust in the Lord and ask him to speak through us, he will.

ACTS 4:8—12

Then Peter, filled with the Holy Spirit, said to them, "Rulers of the people and elders, if we are being examined today concerning a good deed done to a cripple, by what means this man has been healed, be it known to you all, and to all the people of Israel, that by the name of Jesus Christ of Nazareth, whom you crucified, whom God raised from the dead, by him this man is standing before you well. This is the stone which was rejected by you builders, but which has become the cornerstone. And there is salvation in no one else, for there is no other name under heaven given among men by which we must be saved."

Peter's statement about Jesus is utterly central to the gospel. We must always remember that all men and women, boys and girls, are called to Christ. There is no person who is exempt from this call. As we have opportunities to speak with others about our Catholic Faith, we must always maintain the primacy of Christ as Lord and Savior.

There is a prevalent notion that it really doesn't matter whether one is Christian or not, as long as one is a "good person." But as Saint Peter makes clear in this passage, it really *does* matter! "There is salvation in no one else."

ACTS 8:27—31

And [Philip] rose and went. And behold, an Ethiopian, a eunuch, a minister of Candace, the queen of the Ethiopians, in charge of all her treasure, had come to Jerusalem to worship and was returning; seated in his chariot, he was reading the prophet Isaiah. And the Spirit said to Philip, "Go up and join this chariot." So Philip ran to him, and heard him reading

> Isaiah the prophet, and asked, "Do you understand what you are reading?" And he said, "How can I, unless someone guides me?" And he invited Philip to come up and sit with him.

Scripture is sometimes difficult to understand, as Scripture itself tells us, here and elsewhere (see 2 Peter 3:15–17). Without proper guidance from one who knows its authentic meaning, we can easily go astray with faulty interpretation. The Lord sent the deacon Philip to explain to the Ethiopian eunuch the meaning of the biblical text. This is a function of the Church, and it depends on the Holy Spirit's guidance and protection.

Another important dimension of this passage is the miraculous nature of Philip's mission. God made sure that he was *there* for the Ethiopian official. Think of the people in your own life who are far from God. Perhaps they won't listen to you, no matter how loving and patient you might be toward them. For some reason they tune you out. Don't let that discourage you. Remember to pray that the Lord will send a "Philip" to help them.[1]

ACTS 18:9–10

> And the Lord said to Paul one night in a vision, "Do not be afraid, but speak and do not be silent; for I am with you, and no man shall attack you to harm you; for I have many people in this city."

If you commit this verse to memory, it will serve you well when you are tempted to be afraid and timid about speaking about Jesus Christ and the Catholic Church. The Lord will sustain and protect you, just as he did Paul. Take heart and speak out.

ROMANS 1:16—17

For I am not ashamed of the gospel: it is the power of God for salvation to every one who has faith, to the Jew first and also to the Greek. For in it the righteousness of God is revealed through faith for faith; as it is written, "He who through faith is righteous shall live."

This verse is a rallying call to all Catholics, because it reminds us that we should never be timid in proclaiming the gospel of Christ. Respectful and charitable, yes, but never timid.

Countless conversions to Christ and the Catholic Church have come about because everyday Catholics have spoken the truth with courage and conviction. God wants to make use of your voice too. As this passage points out, if you are not ashamed of the gospel, the power of God's truth will radiate from you—sometimes when you don't even say anything—and his righteousness will be revealed through you to those you encounter (see Matthew 5:14–16).

I CORINTHIANS 15:12—22

Now if Christ is preached as raised from the dead, how can some of you say that there is no resurrection of the dead? But if there is no resurrection of the dead, then Christ has not been raised; if Christ has not been raised, then our preaching is in vain and your faith is in vain. We are even found to be misrepresenting God, because we testified of God that he raised Christ, whom he did not raise if it is true that the dead are not raised. For if the dead are not raised, then Christ has not been raised. If Christ has not been raised, your faith is futile and you are still in your sins. Then those also who have fallen asleep in Christ have perished. If for this life only we have hoped in Christ, we are of all men most to be pitied.

But in fact Christ has been raised from the dead, the first fruits of those who have fallen asleep. For as by a man came death, by a man has come also the resurrection of the dead. For as in Adam all die, so also in Christ shall all be made alive.

This passage is quite blunt. If Jesus Christ did not rise from the dead, then he was not God. And if he was not God, he was a fraud. And if he was a fraud, then Christians would be the most pitiable of people. There really is no alternative.

Catholic philosopher and apologist Peter Kreeft explains:

[E]ither (1) the resurrection really happened, (2) the apostles were deceived by a hallucination, (3) the apostles created a myth, not meaning it literally, (4) the apostles were deceivers who conspired to foist on the world the most famous and successful lie in history, or (5) Jesus only swooned and was resuscitated, not resurrected. All five theories are logically possible, and therefore must be fairly investigated—even (1)! They are also the *only* possibilities, unless we include really far-out ideas that responsible historians have never taken seriously, such as that Jesus was really a Martian who came in a flying saucer. Or that he never even existed; that the whole story was the world's greatest fantasy novel, written by some simple fisherman; that he was a literary character whom everyone in history mistook for a real person, including all Christians *and* their enemies, until some scholar many centuries later got the real scoop from sources unnamed.[2]

Kreeft goes on in this article to show how the only logical option, fully consistent with the historically demonstrable facts from pagan, Jewish and Christian sources, is that Christ rose from the dead. And if he rose from the dead, then he *is* indeed God (as he repeatedly claimed to be). And if he is God, then Christians—far from being pitiable—possess a stunning, magnificent, history-altering truth, one that we must share with the world.

PHILIPPIANS 1:27–30

Only let your manner of life be worthy of the gospel of Christ, so that whether I come and see you or am absent, I may hear of you that you stand firm in one spirit, with one mind striving side by side for the faith of the gospel, and not frightened in anything by your opponents. This is a clear omen to them of their destruction, but of your salvation, and that from God. For it has been granted to you that for the sake of Christ you should not only believe in him but also suffer for his sake, engaged in the same conflict which you saw and now hear to be mine.

Saint Paul's beautiful and encouraging words to the Philippians were a premonition of the wave of bloody persecution that the Roman Empire would soon unleash against the Church. Saint Paul himself was beheaded by Nero, circa AD 64.

Saint Paul's words encourage us today to be willing to suffer when necessary for the gospel. Many of us face some kind of persecution in our efforts to speak about Christ, be it only rejection and ridicule rather than physical suffering. Let's stand firm and be faithful witnesses to Jesus Christ and the Catholic Church in our words and in our actions.

COLOSSIANS 4:2–6

Continue steadfastly in prayer, being watchful in it with thanksgiving; and pray for us also, that God may open to us a door for the word, to declare the mystery of Christ, on account of which I am in prison, that I may make it clear, as I ought to speak.

> Conduct yourselves wisely toward outsiders, making the most of the time. Let your speech always be gracious, seasoned with salt, so that you may know how you ought to answer every one.

The Lord's ways are mysterious, and this passage points to the need for prayer to discern the right time and place and words— that is, waiting for God to "open a door"—for proclaiming the truth of Christ and his Church. God alone knows what the right combination is for each person and situation we encounter. We need to pray that he will reveal it.

Relying on the prayers of our fellow Christians and seeking the will of God in all our dealings with people are key to true fidelity to our call as Apostles for Christ. Added to this is the reminder that in all our activities we should shun profane or crude speech, striving to speak graciously and in a charitable and winsome way with all, so that the peace and beauty of the truth will be evident in our words and manner.

I THESSALONIANS 5:14–18

> [W]e exhort you, brethren, admonish the idle, encourage the fainthearted, help the weak, be patient with them all. See that none of you repays evil for evil, but always seek to do good to one another and to all. Rejoice always, pray constantly, give thanks in all circumstances; for this is the will of God in Christ Jesus for you.

If Catholics, not to mention other Christians, really lived by these words, the mission of the Church to evangelize the world would be unstoppable. Instead, the bickering, strife, polarization, mistrust, apathy and lukewarmness that characterize so much of Christianity today is the opposite of what Scripture commands us to do. This is not to say that Saint Paul's teaching is easy to follow, but it is the right way.

To borrow a line from an old song, "Let peace begin with me." If we are to see the kind of harmonious charity described in this passage, we must begin the process in our own hearts.

That's where the kind of harmonious charity Paul describes must begin.

1 PETER 3:14–17

Have no fear of them, nor be troubled, but in your hearts reverence Christ as Lord. Always be prepared to make a defense to any one who calls you to account for the hope that is in you, yet do it with gentleness and reverence; and keep your conscience clear, so that, when you are abused, those who revile your good behavior in Christ may be put to shame. For it is better to suffer for doing right, if that should be God's will, than for doing wrong.

There are two major truths to focus on here. First, if you stand up for the truth of Jesus Christ and his Church, you are bound to be criticized. You might even suffer for your stand. And a few, those we call "martyrs," even shed their blood for the truth.[3]

Each step of heroic witness to the truth requires some kind of sacrifice, as you surely know if you have ever stood up to coworkers or friends who mocked Christ or the Catholic Church's teachings. Perhaps you've suffered scorn in your own family for taking a stand on abortion, euthanasia, contraception or divorce and remarriage. Saint Peter reminds you in this passage to fear not, continue speaking the truth with patience and clarity and know that God will bless you for it.

Also, notice that Saint Peter exhorts us to "always be ready to give a defense." The word for "defense" in Greek is *apología*, from which the word *apologetics* is derived. Regardless of your age, state of life, personality type and so on, you have a call from God to always be ready to stand up for the truth.

Obviously, we should never do this in a haughty, condescending or mean-spirited way. Saint Peter reminds us to engage in apologetics with "gentleness and reverence." *How* we speak is just as crucial as what we say.

CHAPTER 7
The Sacraments

BAPTISM

JOHN 3:2–6

This man [Nicodemus] came to Jesus by night and said to him, "Rabbi, we know that you are a teacher come from God; for no one can do these signs that you do, unless God is with him." Jesus answered him, "Truly, truly, I say to you, unless one is born anew, he cannot see the kingdom of God." Nicodemus said to him, "How can a man be born when he is old? Can he enter a second time into his mother's womb and be born?" Jesus answered, "Truly, truly, I say to you, unless one is born of water and the Spirit, he cannot enter the kingdom of God. That which is born of the flesh is flesh, and that which is born of the Spirit is spirit." (See also 1 Peter 3:18–22.)

This passage reveals how to be "born again" the Bible way. Christ says we must be born of *water* and the Holy Spirit, clearly referring to baptism.

Nicodemus misunderstood Christ's statement about being "born from above," thinking that he meant being born *again* in a physical sense, something that clearly baffled Nicodemus. Christ was referring to baptism: unless you are born of *water* and the Holy Spirit. To be born again in the sense that the Lord meant these words is to be baptized.

Many Scripture passages support this understanding, but one significant clue is found in the same chapter. Immediately after saying these things, Christ went with his Apostles and spent some time *baptizing* (see John 3:22).[1]

ACTS 2:37–39

Now when they heard this they were cut to the heart, and said to Peter and the rest of the Apostles, "Brethren, what shall we do?" And Peter said to them, "Repent, and be baptized every one of you in the name of Jesus Christ for the forgiveness of your sins; and you shall receive the gift of the Holy Spirit. For the promise is to you and to your children and to all that are far off, every one whom the Lord our God calls to him." (See Titus 3:4–7.)

Just before he ascended to the Father, the Lord commanded his Apostles to go forth into the whole world and *baptize* (see Matthew 28:19–20). And here we see them carrying out that command with gusto. Three thousand people were baptized in a single day (Acts 2:41)!

Saint Peter, speaking here on behalf of the entire Church, tells the crowds that through baptism they will receive forgiveness of their sins and the gift of the Holy Spirit. This is precisely what the Catholic Church teaches are the effects of baptism (see *CCC*, 1213, 1215, 1257).

Notice also that there is no age restriction imposed for baptism. This promise is for children as well as adults.

ACTS 16:30–34

[The jailer] said, "Men, what must I do to be saved?" And they said, "Believe in the Lord Jesus, and you will be saved, you and your household." And they spoke the word of the Lord to him and to all that were in his house. And he took them the same hour of the night, and washed their wounds, and he was baptized at once, with all his family. Then he brought them up into his house, and set food before them; and he rejoiced with all his household that he had believed in God.

This amazing passage reminds us of the mighty power of God's grace. The Philippian jailer, when he saw the miracle God had performed to release Paul and Silas from prison, was about to fall on his sword in despair. He knew he would be blamed for their escape and punished with execution. But Paul stopped him. The jailer received salvation through faith in Christ and was baptized for the forgiveness of sins (see Matthew 28:19; Mark 16:16; Acts 2:37–39).

We see here some indications of the Catholic Church's understanding of the sacrament of baptism. The fortunate man and *his whole family*—young and old alike—were baptized that evening. We can be certain that the man did not have a house with the luxury of a large indoor pool of water, jailers being at the low end of the social pecking order. This indicates that the baptisms were almost certainly done by pouring water over the head, not by immersion.

ACTS 22:16

And now why do you wait? Rise and be baptized, and wash away your sins, calling on his name.

Here again we see the sacrament of baptism presented as the doorway into the Church. Saul's conversion to Christ was complete, and the gift of faith was firmly fixed in his heart, but first, Ananias pointed out, he should be baptized.

This text affirms Catholic teaching on the nature of baptism and its effect of washing away sin (see *CCC*, 1213).

CONFIRMATION

ACTS 2:1—4

When the day of Pentecost had come, they were all together in one place. And suddenly a sound came from heaven like the rush of a mighty wind, and it filled all the house where they were sitting. And there appeared to them tongues as of fire, distributed and resting on each one of them. And they were all filled with the Holy Spirit and began to speak in other tongues, as the Spirit gave them utterance.

The Catholic sacrament of confirmation is the continuation of the outpouring of the Holy Spirit, which the Apostles experienced so powerfully on the Day of Pentecost (see *CCC*, 1288, 1302). When the Holy Spirit came down upon them, as they were gathered in the Upper Room, he not only stirred into flame a new level of zeal and boldness for preaching the Good News but also appeared as tongues of flame above their heads. What a marvelous and awesome sight this must have been!

It is well worth remembering that when someone is confirmed, even though we don't see any physical manifestation of the Holy Spirit's descent, he is there, pouring out grace in abundance. And we too, like the Apostles, must go forth and spread the Good News without fear and with burning charity (see 1 Corinthians 9:16).

THE EUCHARIST

MALACHI 1:11

For from the rising of the sun to its setting my name is great among the nations, and in every place incense is offered to my name, and a pure offering; for my name is great among the nations, says the LORD of hosts.

The early Christians understood this prophecy to be fulfilled in the Eucharistic sacrifice.[2] For example, the *Didache*,[3] a first-century document describing basic Christian doctrines and liturgical practices, says:

> On the Lord's own day [that is, Sunday], gather together and break bread and give thanks [Greek: *eucharistésate*], having first confessed your sins so that your sacrifice may be pure [see 1 Corinthians 11:27–32]. But let no one who has a quarrel with a companion join you until they have been reconciled, so that your sacrifice may not be defiled. For this is the sacrifice concerning which the Lord said, "In every place and time offer me a pure sacrifice, for I am a great king, says the Lord, and my name is marvelous among the nations."[4]

Whenever you assist at the Holy Sacrifice of the Mass, rejoice in knowing that you are participating in the ongoing fulfillment of Malachi's prophecy!

JOHN 6:35–40

Jesus said to them, "I am the bread of life; he who comes to me shall not hunger, and he who believes in me shall never thirst. But I said to you that you have seen me and yet do not believe. All that the Father gives me will come to me; and him who comes to me I will not cast out. For I have come down from heaven, not to do my own will, but the will of him who sent me; and this is the will of him who sent me, that I should lose nothing of all that he has given me, but raise it up at the last day. For this is the will of my Father, that every one who sees the Son and believes in him should have eternal life; and I will raise him up at the last day."

Many Jews stopped following Jesus because of this teaching. They understood him to mean literally that they had to eat his flesh and drink his blood. This teaching on the Eucharist is so startling that, even today, many people reject it.

For two thousand years the Catholic Church has continued to proclaim the literal meaning of Christ's words about his being the Bread of Life. He comes to us under the appearances of bread and wine in the Eucharist.

At an allegorical level, we also can see that those who come to Christ in faith will never hunger, and those who believe in him will never thirst. Coming to and believing in the Lord are integral to this passage, and they form a kind of supernatural foundation for the real presence of Christ in the Eucharist.

When we come to receive the Lord in the Eucharist, and when we believe in his real presence, we are believing in something we cannot perceive with our physical senses. And Christ calls "blessed" those who believe even when they cannot see (see John 20:29).

Saint Thomas Aquinas composed this prayer of thanksgiving to the Lord after receiving the Holy Eucharist at Mass:

> LORD, Father all-powerful and ever-living God,
> I thank you, for even though I am a sinner,
> your unprofitable servant,
> not because of my worth
> but in the kindness of your mercy,
> you have fed me with the precious body and blood of
>   your Son,
> our Lord Jesus Christ.
>
> I pray that this holy communion
> may bring me not condemnation and punishment
> but forgiveness and salvation.
> May it be a helmet of faith
> and a shield of good will.
> May it purify me from evil ways
> and put an end to my evil passions.
> May it bring me charity and patience,

humility and obedience,
and growth in the power to do good.
May it be my strong defense
against all my enemies, visible and invisible,
and the perfect calming of all my evil impulses,
bodily and spiritual.
May it unite me more closely to you,
the one true God,
and lead me safely through death
to everlasting happiness with you.

And I pray that you will lead me, a sinner,
to the banquet where you,
with your Son and Holy Spirit,
are true and perfect light,
total fulfillment, everlasting joy,
gladness without end,
and perfect happiness to your saints.

Grant this through Christ our Lord. Amen.[5]

I CORINTHIANS 11:27–29

Whoever, therefore, eats the bread or drinks the cup of the Lord in an unworthy manner will be guilty of profaning the body and blood of the Lord. Let a man examine himself, and so eat of the bread and drink of the cup. For any one who eats and drinks without discerning the body eats and drinks judgment upon himself.

If the Eucharist were not really the body and blood, soul and divinity of Christ under the appearances of bread and wine (see CCC, 1374), why would Saint Paul say these things? His comments would not make sense if the Eucharist were merely a symbol of Christ, which is what many non-Catholics imagine.

The Catholic teaching on the real presence is an expression of this Pauline teaching, which is why the Church instructs non-Catholics not to receive the Body and Blood of the Lord at Mass in Holy Communion. This is not in the least a mean-spirited or divisive request but an immensely loving one. For the Church does not want to see anyone become guilty of "profaning" the sacrament and eating and drinking "judgment" upon himself by receiving Communion when he is unworthy due to serious sin (this rule, of course, extends to all *Catholics* who, because of unconfessed mortal sin, are not worthy to receive Communion) or because they do not recognize the Body and Blood of Christ.

HEBREWS 9:23–28

Thus it was necessary for the copies of the heavenly things to be purified with these rites, but the heavenly things themselves with better sacrifices than these. For Christ has entered, not into a sanctuary made with hands, a copy of the true one, but into heaven itself, now to appear in the presence of God on our behalf. Nor was it to offer himself repeatedly, as the high priest enters the Holy Place yearly with blood not his own; for then he would have had to suffer repeatedly since the foundation of the world. But as it is, he has appeared once for all at the end of the age to put away sin by the sacrifice of himself. And just as it is appointed for men to die once, and after that comes judgment, so Christ, having been offered once to bear the sins of many, will appear a second time, not to deal with sin but to save those who are eagerly waiting for him. (See Hebrews 9:11–14.)

The Old Testament is filled with many "types," that is, fore-shadowings or prefigurements of persons or things in the New Testament. For example, Christ is the fulfillment of the types of Adam and Moses; the Holy Eucharist is a fulfillment of the type of manna, which the Hebrews ate during their wandering in the desert; the ark of the covenant (Exodus 25:10–22) is a type of the Blessed Virgin Mary, who is the Ark of the New Covenant, in that she carried Christ within her.[6]

This passage explains how the Mosaic priesthood is a type of Christ's perfect sacrifice for us. What those priests and their sacrifices only suggested and symbolized, Christ's eternal priesthood and atoning sacrifice perfectly fulfill and accomplish.

What's more, Christ's sacrifice was offered "once for all." The Mass, which is the fulfillment of Christ's command to his Apostles at the Last Supper to "do this in memory of me," is a re-presentation in time and space of that once-for-all sacrifice that he made for us, which he is eternally presenting in heaven to the Father on our behalf.

1 JOHN 3:8

The devil has sinned from the beginning. The reason the Son of God appeared was to destroy the works of the devil.

The works of the devil are his lies. Each time he is successful in tempting us to sin, he accomplishes another deception, just as he did way back in the Garden of Eden (see Genesis 2:15–17, 3:1–7).

Christ, who is the truth, has come to do away with the evil one's reign of deception and its resulting spiritual destruction. And how poetically beautiful it is that, just as eating the fruit of the tree in the Garden poisoned the human race with sin, so eating the fruit of the tree of Calvary—the Holy Eucharist—counteracts this poison with life-giving grace, healing the deadly wound of sin.

Jesus, the New Adam, reverses the catastrophe of the Fall by giving us himself as the Bread of Life. Never forget that. Each time you receive the Holy Eucharist, you participate with the Lord in eradicating the malicious works of the devil.

RECONCILIATION

PSALM 32:1—7

Blessed is he whose transgression is forgiven,
 whose sin is covered.
Blessed is the man to whom the LORD imputes no iniquity,
 and in whose spirit there is no deceit.

When I declared not my sin, my body wasted away
 through my groaning all day long.
For day and night your hand was heavy upon me;
 my strength was dried up as by the heat of summer.

I acknowledged my sin to you,
 and I did not hide my iniquity;
I said, "I will confess my transgressions to the LORD";
 then you forgave the guilt of my sin.

Therefore let every one who is godly
 offer prayer to you;
at a time of distress, in the rush of great waters,
 they shall not reach him.
You are a hiding place for me,
 you preserve me from trouble;
 you surround me with deliverance.

Romans 6:23 warns us that the wages of sin is *death*. Not only does sin lead to eternal death in hell, but also it can lead to physical death or the death of a career, a marriage, a reputation. Living with a guilty conscience also can be deadly.

 The psalmist says that before he confessed his sins to the Lord, his life was miserable. But when he acknowledged his sins with a contrite heart, God delivered him from both the bonds of spiritual death and the misery of a heavy-laden conscience.

If you are not conscious of any serious (that is, mortal) sin on your soul, you can pray this Scripture passage with the grateful joy of one who has turned to God and received forgiveness. Even the "rush of great waters" will not sweep you away, as long as you remain steadfastly united to him (see Matthew 7:24–27; 16:18; Romans 11:20–22).

If, on the other hand, you are huddling in the shadows of unconfessed mortal sin (as Adam and Eve huddled in shame, trying to hide from God after their sin; see Genesis 3:7–10), sick at heart with guilt and tired of being estranged from God's merciful love, you can turn to him right now. Read Psalm 32:1–7 aloud, slowly and prayerfully, and repent of your sins with a sincere and contrite heart. The Lord will forgive you.

Then, as quickly as you can, even today, go to a priest and make a good sacramental confession. God is waiting for you with outstretched arms. Don't delay your return to him.

PSALM 51:1–12

Have mercy on me, O God,
> according to your merciful love;
according to your abundant mercy blot out my transgressions.
Wash me thoroughly from my iniquity,
> and cleanse me from my sin!

For I know my transgressions,
> and my sin is ever before me.
Against you, you only, have I sinned,
> and done that which is evil in your sight,
so that you are justified in your sentence
> and blameless in your judgment.
Behold, I was brought forth in iniquity,
> and in sin did my mother conceive me.

Behold, you desire truth in the inward being;
    therefore teach me wisdom in my secret heart.
Purge me with hyssop, and I shall be clean;
    wash me, and I shall be whiter than snow.
Make me hear joy and gladness;
    let the bones which you have broken rejoice.
Hide your face from my sins,
    and blot out all my iniquities.

Create in me a clean heart, O God,
    and put a new and right spirit within me.
Cast me not away from your presence,
    and take not your holy Spirit from me.
Restore to me the joy of your salvation,
    and uphold me with a willing spirit.

Here again Scripture describes the misery of sin, contrasting it with the ineffable joy and peace that come from repenting and receiving the Lord's forgiveness. The psalmist's statement "My sin is ever before me" is painfully familiar to all of us, especially those who persist in serious sin and avoid the remedy of sacramental confession. This is another way of saying that their conscience is ringing an alarm bell, trying to warn them that they are in a dangerous situation.

But also notice in this passage the wonderful transformation that God's grace brings about in the soul that turns from sin and comes back to him with a contrite heart. The multifaceted metaphor of being cleaned, washed and purged is a powerful image of having the stains and foulness and corruption of sin removed from us.

Picture yourself hot, sweaty and covered with the grime of several days of hard manual work in hot and humid weather. You've been wearing the same filthy clothes the whole time. Your hair is matted and oily. You look bad, and you smell bad, *really* bad. You yearn for a long hot shower and a clean set of clothes.

Now try to imagine someone in this situation who, when the opportunity presents itself, decides not to take a shower and change clothes! He's grown so accustomed to being filthy that it no longer really bothers him. And taking a shower and changing clothes are too much of an inconvenience to bother with.

That's pretty hard to imagine, right? Well, this analogy is a pale comparison to the horrifying effects of sin on the soul and the folly of the Catholic who avoids going to confession because it's a bother. If you think you might be in this category, my advice is to kneel before a crucifix and pray Psalm 51:3–11 out loud, asking God to give you the grace to receive the clean heart he wants so much to create in you. And then go to confession!

JOHN 20:19—23

On the evening of that day, the first day of the week, the doors being shut where the disciples were, for fear of the Jews, Jesus came and stood among them and said to them, "Peace be with you." When he had said this, he showed them his hands and his side. Then the disciples were glad when they saw the Lord. Jesus said to them again, "Peace be with you. As the Father has sent me, even so I send you." And when he had said this, he breathed on them, and said to them, "Receive the Holy Spirit. If you forgive the sins of any, they are forgiven; if you retain the sins of any, they are retained."

Here we see a major scriptural monument to the Catholic teaching on the forgiveness of sins in the sacrament of confession. Notice that while Christ gave his Apostles the power to forgive sins, he did not also give them the ability to read minds. The only way for them to exercise this ministry of reconciliation (see 2 Corinthians 5:18–21) was for penitents to confess their sins to them.

A very important and often overlooked element in this passage is the statement "He *breathed* on them." We see here that, in a particular sense, the Apostles themselves became "God-breathed." This refutes the claim that Scripture is the only thing mentioned in Scripture as "God-breathed" (see 2 Timothy 3:16; Greek: *theopneustos*, translated "inspired" in the *Revised Standard Version Catholic Edition*).[7] The verse also parallels the only other place in Scripture where we see God breathing on someone, in Genesis 2:7. There he gives life to Adam; here he gives power and authority to the Apostles, and through them, to the Catholic Church.

2 CORINTHIANS 5:17–20

Therefore, if any one is in Christ, he is a new creation; the old has passed away, behold, the new has come. All this is from God, who through Christ reconciled us to himself and gave us the ministry of reconciliation; that is, in Christ God was reconciling the world to himself, not counting their trespasses against them, and entrusting to us the message of reconciliation. So we are ambassadors for Christ, God making his appeal through us. We beg you on behalf of Christ, be reconciled to God.

Perhaps you have experienced a tremendous sense of relief and even euphoria after making a good confession. The graces of the sacrament truly invigorate the soul with sentiments of joy and hope and gratitude to the Lord for his loving mercy. This is one reason why the sacrament of confession needs to be "rediscovered" by the many Catholics who have not availed themselves of it adequately. If you want to find peace with God and with yourself, start going to confession frequently. It really works.

And remember that Saint Paul's plaintive request that we be reconciled to God contains a note of urgency. "I *beg* you," he says. Clearly this isn't merely a suggestion; Paul really wants us to do it.

Christ is waiting for you in the sacrament of confession, longing to help you get rid of your sin. You'll be very glad if you go soon! Why delay any longer?

ANOINTING OF THE SICK

ACTS 19:11–12

And God did extraordinary miracles by the hands of Paul, so that handkerchiefs or aprons were carried away from his body to the sick, and diseases left them and the evil spirits came out of them.

Here we see a biblical episode of God's using sacramentals as conduits of his gracious love. The handkerchiefs and aprons in themselves were nothing special, but God allowed mighty works of healing to be brought about through them. This passage points us to the efficacy of Catholic sacramentals, such as blessed oils, crucifixes, holy water, rosaries and so on.[8]

This passage also points us to the healing ministry that Jesus gave the Apostles—and by extension to our bishops and priests today.

JAMES 5:13–16

Is any one among you suffering? Let him pray. Is any cheerful? Let him sing praise. Is any among you sick? Let him call for the elders of the Church, and let them pray over him, anointing him with oil in the name of the Lord; and the prayer of faith will save the sick man, and the Lord will raise him up; and if he has committed sins, he will be forgiven. Therefore confess your sins to one another, and pray for one another, that you may be healed. The prayer of a righteous man has great power in its effects.

Here we see a major scriptural foundation for the Catholic sacrament of anointing of the sick (also known as "extreme unction," "the last rites" and "holy anointing"). The Church has celebrated this sacrament since the days of the early Christians.

Many of us regard this sacrament as a preparation for death, and it does serve this function. The *Catechism* gives a fuller explanation:

> The Anointing of the Sick "is not a sacrament for those only who are at the point of death. Hence, as soon as anyone of the faithful begins to be in danger of death from sickness or old age, the fitting time for him to receive this sacrament has certainly already arrived" [*Sacrosanctum Concilium* 73; cf. Code of Canon Law, canons 1004 § 1, 1005; 1007; CCEO, canon 738].
>
> If a sick person who received this anointing recovers his health, he can in the case of another grave illness receive this sacrament again. If during the same illness the person's condition becomes more serious, the sacrament may be repeated. It is fitting to receive the Anointing of the Sick just prior to a serious operation. The same holds for the elderly whose frailty becomes more pronounced.
>
> ...It is the duty of pastors to instruct the faithful on the benefits of this sacrament. The faithful should encourage the sick to call for a priest to receive this sacrament. The sick should prepare themselves to receive it with good dispositions, assisted by their pastor and the whole ecclesial community, which is invited to surround the sick in a special way through their prayers and fraternal attention.
>
> Like all the sacraments, the Anointing of the Sick is a liturgical and communal celebration [see *Sacrosanctum*

Concilium 73], whether it takes place in the family home, a hospital or church, for a single sick person or a whole group of sick persons. It is very fitting to celebrate it within the Eucharist, the memorial of the Lord's Passover. If circumstances suggest it, the celebration of the sacrament can be preceded by the sacrament of Penance and followed by the sacrament of the Eucharist. As the sacrament of Christ's Passover the Eucharist should always be the last sacrament of the earthly journey, the "viaticum" for "passing over" to eternal life. (CCC, 1514–1517; see CCC, 1499–1532)

HOLY ORDERS

MATTHEW 9:36–38

When he saw the crowds, he had compassion for them, because they were harassed and helpless, like sheep without a shepherd. Then he said to his disciples, "The harvest is plentiful, but the laborers are few; pray therefore the Lord of the harvest to send out laborers into his harvest."

As the old song goes, "Jesus loves me, this I know, for the Bible tells me so." And this is one of those places where the Bible tells us about this great love Jesus has for us.

Notice that he had *compassion* for the crowds. He didn't exclaim, "Oh, how unfortunate!" at their plight of being "like sheep without a shepherd" and then go about his business. No. Christ gave himself for us as our Good Shepherd (see John 10:11–14) and High Priest (Hebrews 8—10), and he calls men to the priesthood to assist him in this work of shepherding the flock.

Perhaps now more than ever, during what is commonly called a "vocations crisis," we would do well to meditate on the final few words of this passage when we pray. The harvest of souls is truly plentiful, but if we don't pray for the few laborers who are already working the harvest and for God to send us more of them, many souls might be lost.

You can become part of the solution to the "vocations crisis" by praying fervently for this intention. If we earnestly "ask," "seek" and "knock," God will answer our prayers and send more laborers into the harvest (Matthew 7:7).

MATTHEW 19:11–12

[Jesus said,] "Not all can accept [this] word, but only those to whom it has been granted. Some are incapable of marriage because they born so; some, because they were made so by others; some, because they have renounced marriage for the sake of the kingdom of heaven. Whoever can accept this ought to accept it." (*NAB*)

To say the least, it's not easy for people these days to appreciate the value of *consecrated* virginity. This is due, in part, to our modern obsession with sex and eroticism. This culture desperately needs models of holiness and self-sacrifice who serve the Lord and his Church with single-minded fidelity.

There are, of course, many practical reasons for celibacy, which Saint Paul alludes to in 1 Corinthians 7:28b, 32–35. Among them is the undeniable reality that married people are consumed with the day-to-day cares of tending to, pleasing and serving their spouses and their children. As any happily married man or woman will testify, marriage is a full-time vocation.

Being a priest entails a universal availability to the Church. It calls for a heroic generosity of self, rising above the good and natural desire for the intimate companionship of a wife, the joy of children and all the other benefits of marriage. Let's not forget that Christ himself said that in heaven there will be no marriage nor giving in marriage (see Matthew 22:30; Luke 20:35), because all the blessed will be nuptially united with the Lord for all eternity, and all good things, including the good of human friendship, will be completed and utterly fulfilled in our union with God.[9]

The beauty of this teaching of Christ is that the members of his body are called to different and mutually complementary services (see 1 Corinthians 12:12–27).

ACTS 1:15–17, 20

In those days Peter stood up among the brethren (the company of persons was in all about a hundred and twenty), and said, "Brethren, the Scripture had to be fulfilled, which the Holy Spirit spoke beforehand by the mouth of David, concerning Judas who was guide to those who arrested Jesus. For he was numbered among us, and was allotted his share in this ministry.... For it is written in the book of Psalms, 'Let his habitation become desolate, and let there be no one to live in it'; and 'His office let another take.'" (See Acts 1:21–26.)

After Judas betrayed Christ and committed suicide, there was a vacancy among the Apostles. Peter, taking the lead, gathered the Apostles so they could choose a replacement for Judas. This is the first link in the chain of apostolic succession in the Church.

Vatican II explained: "Amongst those various offices which have been exercised in the Church from the earliest times the chief place, according to the witness of tradition, is held by the function of those who, through their appointment to the dignity and responsibility of bishop, and in virtue consequently of the unbroken succession, going back to the beginning, are regarded as transmitters of the apostolic line."[10]

1 TIMOTHY 4:11–16

Command and teach these things. Let no one despise your youth, but set the believers an example in speech and conduct, in love, in faith, in purity. Till I come, attend to the public reading of Scripture, to preaching, to teaching. Do not neglect the gift you have, which was given you by prophetic utterance when the council of elders laid their hands upon you. Practice these duties, devote yourself to them, so that all may see your progress. Take heed to yourself and to your teaching; hold to that, for by so doing you will save both yourself and your hearers.

This passage also points us to the doctrine of apostolic succession. Timothy was a young bishop whom Saint Paul chose to carry on his apostolic work. Here Paul reminds him of the authority he has been granted as an *episcopos*—the Greek word for "overseer" that is today rendered in English as *bishop*.

Timothy received from his mentor Paul the blueprint for effective episcopal leadership: He was to teach lovingly but fearlessly. This is the very heavy duty of each Catholic bishop. Would that all bishops took it to heart and acted upon it, and would that all the faithful prayed earnestly and frequently for their bishop.

MATRIMONY

MATTHEW 19:9

I say to you: whoever divorces his wife, except for unchastity, and marries another, commits adultery; and he who marries a divorced woman, commits adultery.

Divorce and remarriage is a huge problem for Christians these days. Practically everyone is affected by it in some way. And while there are many angles from which this issue can be approached, let's focus on the part of this verse commonly called the "exception clause"—where Christ says, "except for unchastity"—because it is here that many people become confused. We need to unpack this verse somewhat to understand what's really being said here.

First, the Lord is clear that any man who divorces his wife (or, in the modern era, a woman who divorces her husband) commits adultery (see CCC, 2384–2386). This is a serious sin. As Saint Paul reminds us in 1 Corinthians 6:9–10, adulterers cannot inherit the kingdom of heaven.[11]

Second, there are situations in which a man and a woman are legally married (that is, in the eyes of the state) in a Church ceremony, but perhaps unbeknownst to one or both of them, there is some kind of impediment that prevents the marriage from being sacramentally valid.[12] This means that, in spite of the marriage's external appearances, including the begetting of children,[13] the marriage was not valid in the eyes of God and is, therefore, materially a situation of *porneia* (Greek: sexual unlawfulness). Keep in mind that one or even both of the spouses may not realize that this is the case, which is why the Church allows for the process of inquiry, after a couple divorces, that may result in a declaration of nullity.

Third, in a situation where the marriage was not valid in the eyes of God, the man and woman are free to marry, because they were not sacramentally married in the first place (see CCC, 1629).

And finally, we come back to the issue of the insolubility of a validly, sacramentally contracted marriage. As the Lord solemnly declared, "What God has joined together, let no man put asunder."

In his encyclical *Familiaris Consortio*, Pope John Paul II quoted the Church Father Tertullian on "the greatness of this conjugal life in Christ and its beauty":

How can I ever express the happiness of the marriage that is joined together by the Church strengthened by an offering, sealed by a blessing, announced by angels and ratified by the Father?... How wonderful the bond between two believers with a single hope, a single desire, a single observance, a single service! They are both brethren and both fellow-servants; there is no separation between them in spirit or flesh; in fact they are truly two in one flesh and where the flesh is one, one is the spirit.[14]

CHAPTER 8
The Communion of Saints

2 KINGS 13:20—21

Elisha died, and they buried him. Now bands of Moabites used to invade the land in the spring of the year. And as a man was being buried, behold, a marauding band was seen and the man was cast into the grave of Elisha; and as soon as the man touched the bones of Elisha, he revived, and stood on his feet.

I cannot begin to guess who was the more astounded by this situation: the men who tossed the body into the tomb, the Moabite bandits or the man who came back to life!

Elisha, a great prophet and a holy man of God, was an instrument of the Lord's grace and blessings during his earthly life and even after his death. This is no surprise to people who understand the Catholic Church's teaching on the nature and meaning of relics. The *Catechism* tells us, "The religious sense of the Christian people has always found expression in various forms of piety..., such as the veneration of relics" (*CCC*, 1674).

JOHN 17:22

The glory which you have given me I have given to them, that they may be one even as we are one.

One hallmark of the Catholic faith is its teaching that God sheds his glory across his creation and in a particular way shares that glory with human beings. The Blessed Virgin Mary and the saints reflect his glory in their love and virtue, as we do too, to the extent that we strive to live in the light of God's grace.

The question is, how well do we receive and radiate God's glory? The person who is lukewarm, feeble in his love for God or, worse yet, steeped in sin will reflect little if any of the glorious visage of the Lord. But the more we imitate Christ by cultivating virtue and deepening our love for and knowledge of God through prayer and the sacraments, the brighter and more magnificently God's grace will radiate from us. If you want to radiate the glory of the Lord more brightly, spend time "polishing the mirror" of your soul with prayer, and stay close to him in the sacraments.

ROMANS 1:9–12

For God is my witness, whom I serve with my spirit in the gospel of his Son, that without ceasing I mention you always in my prayers, asking that somehow by God's will I may now at last succeed in coming to you. For I long to see you, that I may impart to you some spiritual gift to strengthen you, that is, that we may be mutually encouraged by each other's faith, both yours and mine.

What a beautiful passage this is, especially when we remember that just as Saint Paul fervently prayed for others while he was alive, all the more is he now in heaven praying and interceding for us here on earth. This is precisely what the Catholic Church teaches about the communion of saints. The Blessed Virgin Mary and all the saints in heaven have both the ability and the keen desire to assist us here on earth, as well as those in purgatory, with their intercessory prayers.[1]

I CORINTHIANS 11:1—2

Be imitators of me, as I am of Christ. I commend you because you remember me in everything and maintain the traditions even as I have delivered them to you.

For two thousand years the Catholic Church has been holding up the saints as models for emulation. These godly Catholic men and women, boys and girls, displayed admirable faith and virtue, and many of them were heroic to the point of shedding their blood for Christ. This Catholic practice of pondering the lives of the saints and seeking to conform our lives to their shining examples has its roots in this passage, among others.

Saint Paul was not boasting when he offered himself as an example to follow. He was being honest about the grace of God active in him and exhorting us to seek that same grace of holiness in our own lives.

Notice also that Saint Paul praised his early Christian audience for maintaining the *traditions* he had imparted to them. Which means that if we are serious about imitating Saint Paul, we will reject the unbiblical Protestant notion of *sola scriptura*, a "tradition of men" that abandons Sacred Tradition in favor of mere human opinions about the meaning of Scripture.

I CORINTHIANS 12:12—21, 26

For just as the body is one and has many members, and all the members of the body, though many, are one body, so it is with Christ. For by one Spirit we were all baptized into one body—Jews or Greeks, slaves or free—and all were made to drink of one Spirit.

For the body does not consist of one member but of many. If the foot should say, "Because I am not a hand, I do not belong to the body," that would not make it any less a part of the body. And if the ear should say, "Because I am not an eye, I do not belong to the body," that would not make it any less a part of the body. If the whole body were an eye, where would be the hearing? If the whole body were an ear, where would be the sense of smell? But as it is, God arranged the organs in the body, each one of them, as he chose. If all were a single organ, where would the body be? As it is, there are many parts, yet one body. The eye cannot say to the hand, "I have no need of you," nor again the head to the feet, "I have no need of you."... If one member suffers, all suffer together; if one member is honored, all rejoice together.

All the members of the body of Christ are united to him and to all the other members *through* him. This means that both our holiness and our sins affect others.

We also see here that there is only *one* body of Christ, not one on earth and another in heaven. All the saints in heaven are as organically united with us in Christ as they were when they were alive on earth.

This is why no member of the body can say, "I do not need you," to any other member. This teaching is at the heart of the Catholic Church's practice of invoking the intercession of the Blessed Virgin Mary and the saints. Simply put, we need them.[2] To deny this, as some do, is to deny the plain meaning of this passage.

EPHESIANS 2:19—22

So then you are no longer strangers and sojourners, but you are fellow citizens with the saints and members of the household of God, built upon the foundation of the Apostles and prophets, Christ Jesus himself being the cornerstone, in whom the whole structure is joined together

and grows into a holy temple in the Lord; in whom you also
are built into it for a dwelling place of God in the Spirit.

How wonderful it is to realize that we are members of the household of God! As members of his family, we have many rights and privileges but also duties and responsibilities toward the Lord and toward our brothers and sisters in the family of God.

Another beautiful image presented here to depict the corporate unity of the household of God is that of a structure. We are "living stones," Saint Peter says in 1 Peter 2:4–5, which together build up the temple of the Lord, who himself is the cornerstone. This means that each one of us has a vital role to play in building the kingdom and supporting the other members of the household of God.

This is an important reminder to pray and sacrifice for others. We can also be consoled to realize that we have the rest of the family praying for us in our times of danger, difficulty and need.

1 TIMOTHY 2:1–6

First of all, then, I urge that supplications, prayers, intercessions, and thanksgivings be made for all men, for kings and all who are in high positions, that we may lead a quiet and peaceable life, godly and respectful in every way. This is good, and it is acceptable in the sight of God our Savior, who desires all men to be saved and to come to the knowledge of the truth. For there is one God, and there is one mediator between God and men, the man Christ Jesus, who gave himself as a ransom for all.

Protestants often invoke verse 5, "There is one God, and there is one mediator between God and men, the man Christ Jesus," as a refutation of the Catholic teaching on the communion of saints. However, exactly the opposite is the case. Because Christ is the one, sufficient, unique mediator between God and men, we can now—in and through him—do the very things that Saint Paul begins this passage with. We can pray, supplicate, offer thanksgiving and intercede for all people.

When someone comes to you and asks for prayer, you wouldn't think to chide him for not going directly to God. God desires that we should intercede for each other ("for this is *good and pleasing* to God") as a part of his mysterious and loving providence for his people.

Finally, all the members of the body, those in heaven and those on earth, are included in this teaching (see 1 Corinthians 12:21). So it is completely biblical to invoke the intercession of the Blessed Virgin Mary and the saints, as we Catholics do.[3]

HEBREWS 12:1—2

Therefore, since we are surrounded by so great a cloud of witnesses, let us also lay aside every weight, and sin which clings so closely, and let us run with perseverance the race that is set before us, looking to Jesus the pioneer and perfecter of our faith, who for the joy that was set before him endured the cross, despising the shame, and is seated at the right hand of the throne of God.

Sporting events are all the more exciting because of the electric atmosphere among fans in the bleachers. They follow every detail of the game, cheer their favorite team on and groan when things don't go right.

In heaven we have just such a "cheering section" of friends and family. The Blessed Virgin Mary and the saints are praying for us and encouraging us as we make our way toward the finish line in this race of the Christian life. They are the "cloud of witnesses" (Hebrews 12:1) who have run the race and now are actively and intently praying for us to join them up in heaven in the winners' circle (see 2 Timothy 2:5, 4:8; 1 Peter 5:4).

REVELATION 8:3–4

And another angel came and stood at the altar with a golden censer; and he was given much incense to mingle with the prayers of all the saints upon the golden altar before the throne; and the smoke of the incense rose with the prayers of the saints from the hand of the angel before God.

This passage particularly shows how those in heaven (the Church triumphant) act as intercessors and helpers for those of us on earth (the Church militant), as well as for the souls in purgatory (the Church suffering), who will enter heaven after their purification (see 1 Corinthians 3:10–15). We ask God for everything we need, and we also ask his friends for their prayers.

The angel in heaven receives the prayers of all the "saints," specifically the holy ones on earth. The angels can do nothing for us apart from God's will. And Scripture makes clear, in this passage and numerous others, that God indeed wills his angels—pure spirits, mighty ministering servants who carry out his commands and assist in the affairs of human beings—to be involved in the mystery of our worship of him.

Whenever you worship the Lord, offer "supplications" and "thanksgivings" for others (1 Timothy 2:1), knowing that this is pleasing to him and that the saints and angels in heaven joyfully behold and even, when God permits it, participate in your act of lifting your heart and prayers to him. Meditate on this beautiful line from Psalm 141:2 when you think about this, especially when you are at the Holy Sacrifice of the Mass or before the Blessed Sacrament: "Let my prayer rise up as incense, and the lifting up of my hands as an evening sacrifice."[4]

MARY, MOTHER OF GOD

LUKE 1:46–49

Mary said,
"My soul magnifies the Lord,
and my spirit rejoices in God my Savior,
for he has regarded the low estate of his handmaiden.
For behold, henceforth all generations will call me blessed;
for he who is mighty has done great things for me,
and holy is his name."

How wonderful and profoundly beneficial it is to meditate on the example of the Blessed Virgin Mary in Sacred Scripture. She was the *first* Christian, our highest model of holiness and the best example of what it means to love God and be totally willing to do his will (see *CCC*, 2030).

Her words "Henceforth, all generations will call me blessed" are a beautiful reminder of Mary's singular privilege from God. For he chose her from all eternity to be the Mother of Christ, the Son of God. It doesn't get any better than that. (See *CCC*, 484–511.) *Deo Gratias.*

JOHN 2:1–11

On the third day there was a marriage at Cana in Galilee, and the mother of Jesus was there; Jesus also was invited to the marriage, with his disciples. When the wine failed, the mother of Jesus said to him, "They have no wine." And Jesus said to her, "O woman, what have you to do with me? My hour has not yet come." His mother said to the servants, "Do whatever he tells you." Now six stone jars were standing there, for the Jewish rites of purification, each holding twenty or thirty gallons. Jesus said to them, "Fill the jars with water." And they filled them up to the brim. He said to them, "Now draw some out, and take it to the steward of the feast." So they took it. When the steward of the feast tasted the water now become wine, and did not know where it came from (though the servants who had drawn the water knew), the steward of the feast called the bridegroom and said to him, "Every man serves the good wine first; and when men have drunk freely, then the poor wine; but you have kept the good wine until now." This, the first of his signs, Jesus did at Cana in Galilee, and manifested his glory; and his disciples believed in him.

Several fascinating and important things emerge in this text.

First, we see that the very first public miracle Christ performed was the result of the intercession of his Mother, the Blessed Virgin Mary. She saw people in need, and she went to her Son, knowing that he would not deny her request.

Second, we see Christ's curious question to her: "What have you to do with me?" A more literal rendering would be: "What [is this] to you and to me?"

Rather than some kind of rebuke, his words were intended to ask his mother if she truly understood the meaning of her request. One may assume that Mary did not expect him to leave the table, head down to the local Cana mini-market and pick up more wine. She knew that he was able to perform this miracle. And such an action at this time would inaugurate, in a certain sense, his public ministry.

Third, notice Mary's statement to the servants: "Do whatever he tells you." This is precisely her message to all Christians. Look to Jesus, follow Jesus, believe in Jesus, obey Jesus. Anyone who does these things is her spiritual son or daughter (see Revelation 12:17).

JOHN 19:25–27

[S]tanding by the cross of Jesus were his mother, and his mother's sister, Mary the wife of Clopas, and Mary Magdalene. When Jesus saw his mother, and the disciple whom he loved standing near, he said to his mother, "Woman, behold, your son!" Then he said to the disciple, "Behold, your mother!" And from that hour the disciple took her to his own home.

This passage sheds much light on the question of Mary's perpetual virginity. The Catholic Church teaches that Mary had no other children besides Jesus. And some, especially many Protestants, deny this. John 19:25–27 can help us see the matter more clearly.

Notice, first of all, that the Lord, as he was dying on the cross, entrusted his mother to John, who was not a member of the family (recall that John and his brother James were the sons of Zebedee: see Matthew 4:21; 20:20; Mark 3:17). Why, if Mary had given birth to other sons besides Jesus, would the Lord do this? If she had other children, this act would make little sense. But it makes perfect sense if Mary was, as the Catholic Church teaches, a perpetual virgin and, therefore, had no children aside from Jesus.

Notice also that the sister[5] of Mary the mother of Jesus was also present at the foot of the cross. Her name was Mary, and she was married to a man named Clopas. The significance here is that she was the mother of two of the four men who were called the "brothers" of the Lord in Matthew 13:55. Clearly, then, while these men were certainly close relatives, they could not have been the sons of the Blessed Virgin Mary.[6]

In giving Mary to his beloved disciple, Jesus was giving her to all his beloved in the Church. The Holy Virgin is our mother, and she cares for each one of us.

REVELATION 12:1–6, 17

And a great sign appeared in heaven, a woman clothed with the sun, with the moon under her feet, and on her head a crown of twelve stars; she was with child and she cried out in her pangs of birth, in anguish for delivery. And another sign appeared in heaven; behold, a great red dragon, with seven heads and ten horns, and seven diadems upon his heads. His tail swept down a third of the stars of heaven, and cast them to the earth. And the dragon stood before the woman who was about to bear a child, that he might devour her child when she brought it forth; she brought forth a male child, one who is to rule all the nations with a rod of iron, but her child was caught up to God and to his throne, and the woman fled into the wilderness, where she has a place prepared by God, in which to be nourished for one thousand two hundred and sixty days. ... Then the dragon was angry with the woman, and went off to make war on the rest of her offspring, on those who keep the commandments of God and bear testimony to Jesus.

Many mysterious "signs" appear in this passage. We see the ark of the covenant in the preceding verse (Revelation 11:19) and then its New Testament fulfillment in the woman who is about to give birth to Christ. The dragon, who is intent upon devouring both the woman and her son, is furious when his plans are ruined by God's providential protection. This is a perfect description of the drama of salvation, played out as it is, generation after generation, in the lives of all believers.

Notice that in verse 17 all those who have faith in Christ and keep his commandments are children ("offspring") of the woman. The Catholic Church recognizes that the woman can be understood to be the Blessed Virgin Mary, to whom Genesis 3:15 also alludes as the woman whose "seed" would crush the head of the dragon.

PETER, THE ROCK

MATTHEW 16:13–19

Now when Jesus came into the district of Caesarea Philippi, he asked his disciples, "Who do men say that the Son of man is?" And they said, "Some say John the Baptist, others say Elijah, and others Jeremiah or one of the prophets." He said to them, "But who do you say that I am?" Simon Peter replied, "You are the Christ, the Son of the living God." And Jesus answered him, "Blessed are you, Simon Bar-Jona! For flesh and blood has not revealed this to you, but my Father who is in heaven. And I tell you, you are Peter, and on this rock I will build my Church, and the gates of Hades shall not prevail against it. I will give you the keys of the kingdom of heaven, and whatever you bind on earth shall be bound in heaven, and whatever you loose on earth shall be loosed in heaven." (See Matthew 18:18.)

It wasn't until I had the opportunity to visit this holy place, situated in the northeast corner of what is today Israel, that I began to understand some of the deeper meaning of this powerful passage. During Christ's public ministry he often made use of the didactic power of his environment when teaching the crowds. This passage is a prime example.

From time immemorial the place had been known as Panias—named after the shrine that stood there in honor of the Greek god Pan.[7] The most striking feature of this location is the massive reddish rock cliff that rears up well over a hundred feet. The shrine to Pan was situated on top of the cliff.

Herod the Great dethroned that idol and in its place installed a graven image of Caesar Augustus, who was worshipped as a god, at least ostensibly, by the Romans and their subjects. Herod's son Philip Herod, who was tetrarch of the region during the time of Christ (see Matthew 2:16–18; Luke 3:1), sought to curry favor with imperial Rome by building a city at that place. He gave the city the name *Caesarea Philippi*, which can be roughly translated from the Latin as "Caesar's [city] from Philip."

Across the front of the cliff were carved niches into which the locals placed idols to other pagan gods. At the base was a wide, deep and dark cave, out of which flowed waters that made their way downstream to the River Jordan. Most mysterious, at least to the ancient peoples who inhabited this region, were the unfathomable chasms within this cave. People lowered into these pits very long ropes weighted with rocks, but no matter how long the rope, it was never long enough to allow the rock to hit bottom. This is why the cave became known as one of the "gates of Sheol."[8]

The symbolism of this place where Christ said the fateful words to Simon, "Thou art rock, and upon this rock I will build my Church," becomes clear. There in the background loomed that massive rock upon which sat a temple to a false god. What vivid contrast to the living rock of Peter, upon which Christ, who is the true God, would build his Church![9] And the rushing waters that came forth from the cave known as one of the "gates of Sheol" could not erode the rock. When the Lord spoke the words recounted in Matthew 16:18–19, with which he conferred upon Simon the name "Rock" (Greek: *petros*) and promised to entrust him with the "keys of the kingdom of heaven," his Apostles undoubtedly understood their crucial importance. And ever since, the Catholic Church has recognized that *it* is that Church that Christ is building on the unshakeable rock, the rock that not even the gates of hell can overthrow!

JOHN 21:15–17

When they had finished breakfast, Jesus said to Simon Peter, "Simon, son of John, do you love me more than these?" He said to him, "Yes, Lord; you know that I love you." He said to him, "Feed my lambs." A second time he said to him,

"Simon, son of John, do you love me?" He said to him, "Yes, Lord; you know that I love you." He said to him, "Tend my sheep." He said to him the third time, "Simon, son of John, do you love me?" Peter was grieved because he said to him the third time, "Do you love me?" And he said to him, "Lord, you know everything; you know that I love you." Jesus said to him, "Feed my sheep."

Peter denied Christ three times during the Lord's passion. So it is beautifully poetic that Christ would call him to make a profession of faith three times, once for each of his denials.

In this passage we also see Christ making Peter the shepherd of the flock in a unique way among the Apostles. Only to Peter does the Lord give this command to feed his sheep. This is one of the passages that point us to the unique role of leadership Saint Peter had among the twelve.[10]

GALATIANS 2:11–14

But when Cephas came to Antioch I opposed him to his face, because he stood condemned. For before certain men came from James, he ate with the Gentiles; but when they came he drew back and separated himself, fearing the circumcision party. And with him the rest of the Jews acted insincerely, so that even Barnabas was carried away by their insincerity. But when I saw that they were not straightforward about the truth of the gospel, I said to Cephas before them all, "If you, though a Jew, live like a Gentile and not like a Jew, how can you compel the Gentiles to live like Jews?"

This might seem to be a puzzling passage. Paul rebuked Peter for "fearing the circumcision party," that is, those who believed Christians had to observe Jewish laws and customs, such as circumcision and kosher food regulations. It's puzzling because, as we see in Acts 16:1–5, Paul had his gentile protégé Timothy circumcised lest he rile the Jews they encountered on their apostolic journey. It seems as if Paul is doing the very thing for which he criticized Peter! The deeper meaning seems to be that even Saint Peter, the chief of the Apostles, was not beyond being corrected for acting in a way that was inconsistent with the truth.

CHAPTER 9
Trials and Temptations

[The serpent] said to the woman, "Did God say, 'You shall not eat of any tree of the garden'?" And the woman said to the serpent, "We may eat of the fruit of the trees of the garden; but God said, 'You shall not eat of the fruit of the tree which is in the midst of the garden, neither shall you touch it, lest you die.'" But the serpent said to the woman, "You will not die. For God knows that when you eat of it your eyes will be opened, and you will be like God, knowing good and evil." So when the woman saw that the tree was good for food, and that it was a delight to the eyes, and that the tree was to be desired to make one wise, she took of its fruit and ate; and she also gave some to her husband, and he ate. Then the eyes of both were opened, and they knew that they were naked.

Those who are old enough to remember *The Flip Wilson Show*, a TV comedy from the early seventies, will remember his character "Geraldine," whose trademark line, "The devil made me do it!" became a household phrase.

Well, it's not true that the devil can make you do something evil, but he certainly will try to tempt you to do it. And if the long and miserable history of human sinfulness has shown us anything, it is that Satan is extraordinarily skilled at tempting us. That, and we humans are extraordinarily stupid when we listen to him. Take, for example, what happened in the Garden of Eden.

Here in Genesis 3 we see the beginning of his career as a deceiver and the folly of the first woman and man to believe him (with catastrophic consequences for the rest of the human race; see Romans 5:12). As the Lord reminds us, "He was a murderer from the beginning, and has nothing to do with the truth, because there is no truth in him. When he lies, he speaks according to his own nature, for he is a liar and the father of lies" (John 8:44).

Notice his lie: "Did God *really* tell you not to do this? Come on. He just doesn't want you to have any fun." Satan wants you to think that God is somehow ripping you off by telling you what you should and should not do. But of course, the exact opposite is true. The Lord wants us to be truly free, living in the light of truth, not slaves to sin, hiding in the darkness, ashamed of the nakedness of our slavery. Much like a loving human father who admonishes his young son not to play with matches because the boy could burn the house down and hurt (or kill) himself and others in the process, the moral precepts he gives us are for our own benefit and protection.

Notice also that we are tempted through our senses appetites and imagination.[1] Eve saw that the fruit was good and "a delight to the eyes." This is a reminder of why, when temptations come our way, we must pray to God for strength and keep a tight rein on the imagination so it can't run away with us. The moment we allow ourselves to become beguiled by the devil's lies, wrapped up as they always are in very pretty wrapping paper, we are very close to falling into sin.

EXODUS 14:13–14

And Moses said to the people, "Fear not, stand firm, and see the salvation of the LORD, which he will work for you today; for the Egyptians whom you see today, you shall never see again. The LORD will fight for you, and you have only to be still."

Sometimes in life it might seem as if your troubles are about to overwhelm you. Money problems, difficulties at work, troubled relationships, health challenges and other problems can rise as a single looming tidal wave of adversity that threatens to crash down and ruin everything.

Take heart. The Lord will not abandon you, no matter how difficult—even desperate—things may be. Our God is a God of miracles. Sometimes, according to his all-wise and all-loving divine providence, he saves his miracles for the very last minute. Just think, for example, about the dramatic, edge-of-your-seat story of Abraham and Isaac in Genesis 22!

So when that tidal wave of adversity rises up in your life, call upon the Lord with a faithful heart. Trust in his mercy, and wait upon his grace to buoy you up. He *will* fight for you. You have only to be still.

JOSHUA 1:9

Be strong and of good courage; be not frightened, neither be dismayed; for the LORD your God is with you wherever you go.

There are many things in life that frighten us. War, terrorism, accidents, poverty, violence, natural disasters, hardship, disease, death—the list goes on. We fear many things that are beyond our control. But none of them are beyond God's control. As this verse says, he is with us wherever we go. He loves us and wants what is best for us. Sometimes what is best involves suffering or uncertainty, though we almost always can't see why in the here and now. In heaven all will become clear, but in the meantime we are called to trust in the Lord and live each day, no matter the circumstances, knowing that we are secure in his love, come what may.

Once, when one of my sons was about three years old, one of his neighborhood friends accidentally swung a toy at his face, delivering a deep gash just above the eye. Amid the blood, our son's screams of pain and fear and our own anxiety, my wife and I rushed him to the emergency room for stitches. It would be a major understatement to say that the procedure was not pleasant. Although our little boy didn't understand at that time why his mommy and daddy were allowing the doctor to do painful things to him, like clean and sterilize the gaping wound and then stitch it closed, when he got older it made sense to him. Indeed, now, as an adult, he has just barely a hint of a scar to show for it, and for that he's *very* thankful that we brought him for stitches.

You see, just as God allows us to experience things that involve suffering (sometimes even a *lot* of suffering), my wife and I allowed our son to go through this painful and frightening (for a three-year-old) treatment because it was *better for him* that he do so. Having his injury treated was far better than leaving him untreated and disfigured for life.

In the same way, knowing that God is your loving Father, strive to live out the message of this verse by being strong and of good courage when the troubles of this life arise. The Lord will take care of you.

PSALM 27:1—3

The LORD is my light and my salvation;
　　whom shall I fear?
The LORD is the stronghold of my life;
　　of whom shall I be afraid?

When evildoers assail me,
　　to devour my flesh,
my adversaries and foes,
　　they shall stumble and fall.

Though a host encamp against me,
　　my heart shall not fear;

> though war arise against me,
>> yet I will be confident.

Saint Paul captured the essence of this beautiful psalm when he exulted in Romans 8:31, "If God is for us, who is against us?"

Notice that the psalmist does not say that those who love God will not be assailed, slandered or persecuted. Such trials come, especially to those who love God intensely, as the lives of the great saints testify. But what of it? As Scripture reminds us, all that really matters is that we remain close to the Lord. He will protect us in all the ways that truly matter. Trust in him, and don't worry about what evil may come your way.

PSALM 140:1–4

> Deliver me, O LORD, from evil men;
>> preserve me from violent men,
> who plan evil things in their heart,
>> and stir up wars continually.
> They make their tongue sharp as a serpent's,
>> and under their lips is the poison of vipers.
>
> Guard me, O LORD, from the hands of the wicked;
>> preserve me from violent men,
>> who have planned to trip up my feet.

On September 11, 2001, the world was roughly awakened to the horrifying reality that a new age of terrorism had dawned. The murderous attacks carried out against Americans that day by nineteen Muslim hijackers would be followed by equally heinous terror attacks in Bali (October 12, 2002), Madrid (March 11, 2004) and London (July 7, 2005), resulting in the death and maiming of thousands more victims. There is nothing to indicate that such religiously motivated terrorist acts will cease anytime soon. The fact is, we live in an era in which the threat of terrorism looms over everyone, everywhere.

In dire times like these, the prayer of Psalm 140:1–4 is especially meaningful and useful. Because there *are* evil and violent men lurking out there with evil things in their hearts, seeking to hurt and kill as many innocent people as they can, now more than ever we should call upon the name of the Lord for protection. Pray this prayer not only for yourself and your family but for the safety of all those who, because of their occupations, are daily in situations and places where they are vulnerable to the evil of terrorism—such as airline pilots, policemen and firefighters. People of all walks of life everywhere are at risk, of course, so we ask the Lord for his protection for all.

And let us not forget to pray for the conversion of the terrorists themselves. As steeped as they are in hatred and violence, as long as they are alive, they are not beyond God's mercy and grace. May the Lord grant them conversion of heart.

MATTHEW 5:10–12

Blessed are those who are persecuted for righteousness' sake, for theirs is the kingdom of heaven.

Blessed are you when men revile you and persecute you and utter all kinds of evil against you falsely on my account.

Rejoice and be glad, for your reward is great in heaven, for so men persecuted the prophets who were before you.

Being attacked for your faith in Jesus Christ is certainly not enjoyable, in the natural sense of the word, but it is a cause for joy. Christ here promises that when we are assailed for our belief in him and his teachings, we are, really and truly, accompanying him on the *via dolorosa*, standing with him through his sufferings, taking our place at the foot of the cross. The reason for our joy is not the suffering itself but rather the great and wonderful good that God will bring out of that suffering. In the end there is a magnificent reward waiting in heaven for those who love him (see 1 Corinthians 2:9).

JOHN 15:18–21

If the world hates you, know that it has hated me before it hated you. If you were of the world, the world would love its own; but because you are not of the world, but I chose you out of the world, therefore the world hates you. Remember the word that I said to you, "A servant is not greater than his master." If they persecuted me, they will persecute you; if they kept my word, they will keep yours also. But all this they will do to you on my account, because they do not know him who sent me.

The New Testament lays out in graphic detail how Christ was persecuted and eventually put to death for the truth. We can see in that description a blueprint for the Christian life. We too will run into various types of persecution, opposition, rejection and (for some) even death for the sake of Jesus Christ.

Whether these things come your way in small or large doses, do not be afraid of them. Come what may, Christ will be with you to strengthen and encourage you. And any suffering you might endure for his sake will be repaid in eternal glory, joy, peace and happiness beyond your wildest imagination.

Of course, our fidelity shouldn't be based on rewards but on love for God. And that love will grow as we continue to be faithful. This is our greatest reward.

JOHN 16:33

I have said this to you, that in me you may have peace. In the world you have tribulation; but be of good cheer, I have overcome the world.

What a marvelous verse to commit to memory and ponder in your heart, each and every day of your life! No doubt you will experience troubles: illness, financial setbacks, strife, confrontations, loneliness. Life is difficult; there is no way around it. But keep your eyes fixed on Jesus, and these troubles will pale to insignificance. They are passing away, soon (in the context of eternity anyway) to be forgotten.

Jesus Christ has conquered death and evil. He wants you to share in his victory by being faithful to him in spite of life's hardships. Then you can enjoy eternal peace and happiness with him in heaven. Such a deal!

The great saints understood this passage, and they put it into practice in their daily lives. Saint Teresa of Avila wrote in her breviary:

> Let nothing disturb thee,
> Nothing affright thee;
> All things are passing;
> God never changeth;
> Patient endurance
> Attaineth to all things;
> Who God possesseth
> In nothing is wanting;
> Alone God sufficeth.[2]

You can live this reality if you let Jesus help you. Just ask him to.

ROMANS 8:31–39

What then shall we say to this? If God is for us, who is against us? He who did not spare his own Son but gave him up for us all, will he not also give us all things with him? Who shall bring any charge against God's elect? It is God who justifies; who is to condemn? Is it Christ Jesus, who died, yes, who was raised from the dead, who is at the right hand of God, who indeed intercedes for us? Who shall separate us from the love of Christ? Shall tribulation, or distress, or persecution, or famine, or nakedness, or peril, or sword? As it is written,

> "For your sake we are being killed all the day long;
> we are regarded as sheep to be slaughtered."

No, in all these things we are more than conquerors through him who loved us. For I am sure that neither death, nor life, nor angels, nor principalities, nor things present, nor things to come, nor powers, nor height, nor depth, nor anything else in all creation, will be able to separate us from the love of God in Christ Jesus our Lord.

You might suffer many ordeals for the sake of Christ, but nothing that the world, the flesh or the devil throws at you can separate you from the Lord. The only one that can do that is you.

Because God created you with freedom, and he respects that freedom because he loves you, you have the ability to turn away from him and choose your will over his. But stop and think about the folly of turning your back on the God who loves you more than you can imagine and wants to give you all good. When I put it *that* way, don't sin and rebellion against God look ridiculous and unthinkable? This is where we see the deception of the evil one for what it really is: a counterfeit.

Saint Paul tells us here that we "more than conquer" through the sufferings we endure for the cause of righteousness and fidelity to the Lord. Fear not. Stand strong, come what may. Be faithful, and you will conquer.

I CORINTHIANS 10:6–13

Now these things are warnings for us, not to desire evil as they did. Do not be idolaters as some of them were; as it is written, "The people sat down to eat and drink and rose up to dance." We must not indulge in immorality as some of them did.... These things happened to them as a warning, but they were written down for our instruction, upon whom the end of the ages has come. Therefore let any one who thinks that he stands take heed lest he fall. No temptation has overtaken you that is not common to man. God is faithful, and he will not let you be tempted beyond your strength, but with the temptation will also provide the way of escape, that you may be able to endure it.

This passage reminds us that we must resist the temptations of the world, the flesh and the devil, lest we lose our salvation. Paul warns us not to forget or deny the fact that we can fall, but he also assures us that God will provide all the help we need to stand firm for him.

The Council of Trent echoed Paul's teaching in its "Decree on Justification":

He that shall persevere to the end, he shall be saved, which cannot be obtained from anyone except from Him who is able to make him stand who stands, that he may stand perseveringly, and to raise him who falls, let no one promise himself herein something as certain with an absolute certainty, though all ought to place and repose the firmest hope in God's help. For God, unless men themselves fail in His grace, as he has begun a good work, so will he perfect it, working [in them] to will and to accomplish. Nevertheless, let those who think themselves to stand, take heed lest they fall, and with fear and trembling work out their salvation, in labors, in watchings, in almsdeeds, in prayer, in fastings and chastity. For knowing that they are born again unto the hope of glory, and not as yet unto glory, they ought to fear for the combat that yet remains with the flesh, with the world and with the devil, in which they cannot be victorious unless they be with the grace of God obedient to the Apostle who says, We

*are debtors, not to the flesh, to live according to the flesh; for
if you live according to the flesh, you shall die; but if by the
spirit you mortify the deeds of the flesh, you shall live.* ³

2 CORINTHIANS 4:7–11

But we have this treasure in earthen vessels, to show that the
transcendent power belongs to God and not to us. We are
afflicted in every way, but not crushed; perplexed, but not
driven to despair; persecuted, but not forsaken; struck down,
but not destroyed; always carrying in the body the death of
Jesus, so that the life of Jesus may also be manifested in our
bodies. For while we live we are always being given up to
death for Jesus' sake, so that the life of Jesus may be manifested in our mortal flesh.

In his characteristically vivid and compelling style, Saint Paul
here speaks a great truth about our human condition: Not only
has God endowed our frail bodies with an intellect and will
that reflect his own image and likeness (this would be treasure
enough!), but he also has deigned to manifest in our bodies the
saving mystery of Christ's life and death.

Many volumes could be written by learned theologians on
this one theme. Let it suffice for us to meditate on this passage
as a sign of God's love for his material creation and, in particular, for human beings. And let us never forget that, as Scripture
so often reminds us, our bodies are temples of the Holy Spirit:
God literally dwells within us.

This profound mystery of God's nearness to our weakness
should be the source of immense encouragement and consolation
when life seems bleak. As Saint Paul says, we may be perplexed
and afflicted with suffering in this life, but we never despair,
because God, who loves us, will never forsake us.

EPHESIANS 6:11–17

Put on the whole armor of God, that you may be able to stand against the wiles of the devil. For we are not contending against flesh and blood, but against the principalities, against the powers, against the world rulers of this present darkness, against the spiritual hosts of wickedness in the heavenly places. Therefore take the whole armor of God, that you may be able to withstand in the evil day, and having done all, to stand. Stand therefore, having fastened the belt of truth around your waist, and having put on the breastplate of righteousness, and having shod your feet with the equipment of the gospel of peace; besides all these, taking the shield of faith, with which you can quench all the flaming darts of the Evil One. And take the helmet of salvation, and the sword of the Spirit, which is the word of God.

It's easy to see why this passage has been such a rousing favorite among Christians for nearly two thousand years. We need to be well prepared for combat with the devil; it would be folly to join the battle if we were not fully protected by God's grace. Just before this Saint Paul exhorts us to "be strong in the Lord" (Ephesians 6:10). So it is to the Lord, not to ourselves, that we look for protection.

Saint John Chrysostom said:

He says not, against the fightings, nor against the hostilities, but against the "wiles." For this enemy is at war with us, not simply, nor openly, but by "wiles." What is meant by wiles? To use "wiles," is to deceive and to take by artifice or contrivance; a thing which takes place both in the case of the arts, and by words, and actions, and stratagems, in the case of those who seduce us. I mean something like this. The Devil never proposes to us sins in their proper colors; he does not speak of idolatry, but he sets it off in another dress, using "wiles," that is, making his discourse plausible, employing disguises. Now therefore the Apostle is by this means both rousing the soldiers, and making them vigilant, by persuading and instructing them, that our conflict is with one skilled in the arts of war, and with one who wars not simply, nor directly, but with much wiliness.... [Saint Paul says:] "Let us put on the whole armor of God." Do you see how he banishes all fear? For if it be possible "to do all, and to stand," his describing in detail the power of the enemy does not create cowardice and fear, but it shakes off indolence.[4]

COLOSSIANS 1:24–25

Now I rejoice in my sufferings for your sake, and in my flesh I complete what is lacking in Christ's afflictions for the sake of his body, that is, the Church, of which I became a minister according to the divine office which was given to me for you, to make the word of God fully known.

Perhaps when you were growing up, your mother would tell you to "offer it up" when you stubbed your toe or skinned your knee. She was referring to the doctrine of redemptive suffering: Our human sufferings, endured patiently out of love for God, are united to the perfect suffering of Christ on the cross.

Saint Paul here speaks about how his sufferings assist the Church as a whole. He most certainly did not intend to imply that Christ did not suffer enough! Far from it. Rather, he was explaining that our sufferings have value in God's eyes, and they can assist others, according to God's loving providence, when they are offered to him in a spirit of love and solidarity with the body of Christ. Saint Peter too tells us to offer "spiritual sacrifices" to God (1 Peter 2:5).

2 TIMOTHY 3:1—5

But understand this, that in the last days there will come times of stress. For men will be lovers of self, lovers of money, proud, arrogant, abusive, disobedient to their parents, ungrateful, unholy, inhuman, implacable, slanderers, profligates, fierce, haters of good, treacherous, reckless, swollen with conceit, lovers of pleasure rather than lovers of God, holding the form of religion but denying the power of it. Avoid such people. (See 2 Timothy 4:3—4.)

This passage could have been written—and perhaps it was—about our present time and this present darkness. There is no way of knowing, of course, if we live in the "last days," but it is advisable to live *as if we were.* For even if the end of the world is a thousand years or more in the future, living fervently for Christ can help counteract the terrible things revealed in this text.

There's no point in dwelling on all the evil things described here. Let's zero in on the final line, where Saint Paul exhorts us to stay free as much as possible from people whose sinful attitudes and actions could have a negative effect on us. If you go into a smoky room, even for just a short time, you come out smelling of smoke. In the same way, if you hang out with sinful people, you can't help but be negatively influenced by them.

Sometimes this can be easier said than done. Sometimes these are people within our own families. We need wisdom in handling such situations.

Yes, I know that Jesus dined with sinners, but keep in mind a very important difference between Jesus and you: He is God, and you are not. I say this not to be flippant but to underscore Saint Paul's point. Sometimes avoiding temptation means avoiding sinful people who drag you down.

I PETER 4:12-16, 19

Beloved, do not be surprised at the fiery ordeal which comes upon you to prove you, as though something strange were happening to you. But rejoice in so far as you share Christ's sufferings, that you may also rejoice and be glad when his glory is revealed. If you are reproached for the name of Christ, you are blessed, because the spirit of glory and of God rests upon you. But let none of you suffer as a murderer, or a thief, or a wrongdoer, or a mischief-maker; yet if one suffers as a Christian, let him not be ashamed, but under that name let him glorify God....

Therefore let those who suffer according to God's will do right and entrust their souls to a faithful Creator.

This passage has particular importance during these times of rampant sexual scandals among Catholic priests, as well as the less publicized scandals caused by lay Catholics (think, pro-abortion "Catholic" politicians, publicly dissenting "Catholic" celebrities and so on).[5] All human beings are prone to sin.

We fall into the quicksand of sensuality and wickedness if not for the grace of God. Peter reminds us that we can bring reproach and opprobrium upon ourselves—and even upon Christ and the Catholic Church!—through our own wickedness. We have to stay close to Christ and strive to avoid sin, so that we may never do things that are deserving of derision and reviling from the world.

Notice also Saint Peter's reminder that the "fiery ordeals" of suffering that God sometimes calls us to endure should not surprise us. God's often mysterious providence allows for such sufferings, for our own good and that of others, baffling as that may be. Those who entrust themselves with childlike trust to the Lord's providence will not be disappointed, and their sufferings will gain great merit for them in God's eyes.

CHAPTER 10
The Law of Love

DEUTERONOMY 6:4–6

Hear, O Israel: The LORD our God is one LORD; and you shall love the LORD your God with all your heart, and with all your soul, and with all your might. And these words which I command you this day shall be upon your heart; and you shall teach them diligently to your children, and shall talk of them when you sit in your house, and when you walk by the way, and when you lie down, and when you rise.

Loving God with all one's heart, mind and soul is the foundation of the Christian life. Imagine how truly blessed and holy and spiritually united Catholic families would be if parents taught this profoundly important passage diligently to their children and meditated on its message, coming and going, throughout the day. Imagine how wonderfully different the world would be if all Catholics everywhere took this passage seriously.

Happily, for you and your family, it's not too late to start. As the shoe commercial so aptly puts it, all you have to do is just *do it*. What's holding you back?

Just as no builder would attempt to construct a house without first laying a strong, stable foundation, attempting to build your spiritual life on anything other than the foundation of loving God completely is an invitation to trouble. But if you are truly seeking to love God and trust in his mercy and providence, then you are on your way to heaven (see Matthew 7:24–27).

As the great saints of the past two thousand years have shown us, loving God with one's *whole* heart means surrendering

everything to him: finances, relationships, fertility, job, possessions, everything. If their holy lives have proved anything, it is
that God will not be outdone in generosity. "God is able to provide you with every blessing in abundance, so that you may
always have enough of everything and may provide in abundance for every good work" (2 Corinthians 9:6–15).

MATTHEW 10:37–39

> He who loves father or mother more than me is not worthy of
> me; and he who loves son or daughter more than me is not wor-
> thy of me; and he who does not take his cross and follow me is
> not worthy of me. He who finds his life will lose it, and he who
> loses his life for my sake will find it.

As the inimitable Archbishop Fulton J. Sheen put it, "To every
Christian...there comes the supreme moment when he must
choose between temporal pleasure and eternal freedom. In
order to save our souls, we must often run the risk of losing our
bodies."[1]

This is part of the paradox of the Faith. All the good things
God has given us—parents, family, homes, money, material
success and so on—are secondary to loving God.

Think about Jesus, who is our perfect model. As a man, he
loved this earthly life in the right way. He loved his parents, his
relatives and his friends. We know that he wept at the news of
the death of his friend Lazarus (see John 11:35). No doubt he
enjoyed the taste and satisfaction of a good meal and a refresh-
ing goblet of wine. He certainly enjoyed pleasant weather and
the rest that comes from a sound night's sleep.

As we know from Scripture, Jesus was like us in all things
except sin.[2] So we follow his holy example. In spite of his
wholesome and moderate enjoyment of the good things in this
life, he showed us by his life, sufferings and death what it

means to truly love God above all things, especially when that means being willing to carry our own crosses and follow him.

MATTHEW 22:35—40

One of them, a lawyer, asked him a question, to test him. "Teacher, which is the great commandment in the law?" And he said to him, "You shall love the Lord your God with all your heart, and with all your soul, and with all your mind. This is the great and first commandment. And a second is like it, You shall love your neighbor as yourself. On these two commandments depend all the law and the prophets."

It's truly amazing how much rich theological truth is packed into this brief Scripture passage. Christ here expresses his new covenant law of love in its fullest form. Note well what he says: If you truly love God, you will love others for his sake—not selfishly (with your own interests in mind), not partially (so as not to cost yourself anything), not ostentatiously (so that others will see and admire you).

Saint Paul echoed this theme. When we bear one another's burdens, he wrote, we "fulfil the law of Christ" (Galatians 6:2).

Understanding this central truth unlocks all the major teaching of Scripture, from the Ten Commandments to the Sermon on the Mount, from the beginning of Jesus' public ministry at the Cana wedding to its culmination in his passion, death, resurrection and ascension into heaven. Love is what it's all about.

JOHN 15:9—17

As the Father has loved me, so have I loved you; abide in my love. If you keep my commandments, you will abide in my love, just as I have kept my Father's commandments and abide in his love. These things I have spoken to you, that my joy may be in you, and that your joy may be full.

This is my commandment, that you love one another as I have loved you. Greater love has no man than this, that a man lay down his life for his friends. You are my friends if you do what I command you. No longer do I call you servants, for the servant does not know what his master is doing; but I have called you friends, for all that I have heard from my Father I have made known to you. You did not choose me, but I chose you and appointed you that you should go and bear fruit and that your fruit should abide; so that whatever you ask the Father in my name, he may give it to you. This I command you, to love one another.

It's a tragedy of truly enormous proportions that some people have ripped the vital role of good works out of Christ's teaching about salvation. Jesus Christ commands us to love one another, and this takes the form of feeding the hungry, clothing the naked and so on (see Matthew 25:31–46). To deny or downplay this part of the gospel is to badly misunderstand it (see Romans 2:6–13).

Don't make this grievous mistake (see 2 Peter 3:15–17). Recognize that your faith *and* your good works, done in Christ, are gifts of grace that God gives you and that you receive by faith. God intends these gifts of grace to be active in your life. He wants you to live your faith in Jesus through good works done in grace. This is the heart of this passage.

ROMANS 12:9—21

Let love be genuine; hate what is evil, hold fast to what is good; love one another with brotherly affection; outdo one another in showing honor. Never flag in zeal, be aglow with the Spirit, serve the Lord. Rejoice in your hope, be patient in tribulation, be constant in prayer. Contribute to the needs of the saints, practice hospitality.

Bless those who persecute you; bless and do not curse them. Rejoice with those who rejoice, weep with those who weep. Live in harmony with one another; do not be haughty, but associate with the lowly; never be conceited. Repay no one evil for evil, but take thought for what is noble in the sight of all. If possible, so far as it depends upon you, live peaceably with all. Beloved, never avenge yourselves, but leave it to the wrath of God; for it is written, "Vengeance is mine, I will repay, says the Lord." No, "if your enemy is hungry, feed him; if he is thirsty, give him drink; for by so doing you will heap burning coals upon his head." Do not be overcome by evil, but overcome evil with good.

One could write volumes of commentary on this one passage, but let's concentrate on a few key points.

First, true Christian fellowship is based on charity: a charity that puts others first and self last; a charity that is self-effacing and quick to praise the good in others; a charity that is humble, patient, loving, empathetic, yet strong and decisive. These are the marks of a true Christian.

Second, true charity often involves suffering. Even when others wrong us, we are to seek their good. And the payoff is presented here quite clearly: We will overcome evil with good.

This is the heart of the Good News. God's grace is more powerful than sin—ours or anyone else's.

ROMANS 14:15—19

If your brother is being injured by what you eat, you are no longer walking in love. Do not let what you eat cause the ruin of one for whom Christ died. So do not let what is good to you be spoken of as evil. For the kingdom of God is not food and drink but righteousness and peace and joy in the Holy Spirit; he who thus serves Christ is acceptable to

> God and approved by men. Let us then pursue what makes
> for peace and for mutual upbuilding.

One virtue in short supply these days is charity, which the Bible declares "the greatest" of all the virtues (1 Corinthians 13:13). Being charitable in the authentic sense of the word is often a daunting task. Our human weaknesses tempt us to give of ourselves only partially (not till it hurts), to forgive but never forget, to not let anyone get the upper hand on us. These worldly attitudes are contrary to the message of Jesus Christ.

As Saint Paul says, we are to pursue what will build people up, not tear them down. Let's face it, we all are tempted to look out for number one now and again. Next time that happens to you, read Romans 14:15–19 slowly and prayerfully, asking God to give you the graces of charity and patience. Take a deep breath, and then go do the right thing.

I CORINTHIANS 13:1–7

> If I speak in the tongues of men and of angels, but have not love, I am a noisy gong or a clanging cymbal. And if I have prophetic powers, and understand all mysteries and all knowledge, and if I have all faith, so as to remove mountains, but have not love, I am nothing. If I give away all I have, and if I deliver my body to be burned, but have not love, I gain nothing.
>
> Love is patient and kind; love is not jealous or boastful; it is not arrogant or rude. Love does not insist on its own way; it is not irritable or resentful; it does not rejoice at wrong, but rejoices in the right. Love bears all things, believes all things, hopes all things, endures all things.

This Bible verse is hugely popular as a reading at weddings, and for good reason. Love is at the foundation of a good marriage.

But notice that Saint Paul identifies the theological virtue of charity—in all its aspects—as the preeminent virtue for *all* Christians, not just newlyweds.

Are you having trouble in a relationship? It helps to meditate on these words of Saint Paul and seek to apply them to your daily life. You'll eventually see amazing results.

As you grow in the virtue of charity, the other virtues will grow in you along with it. You will become ever more conformed to the image of Jesus Christ and ever more ready to meet him on that day when he calls you to your heavenly reward.

2 CORINTHIANS 9:6–8

[H]e who sows sparingly will also reap sparingly, and he who sows bountifully will also reap bountifully. Each one must do as he has made up his mind, not reluctantly or under compulsion, for God loves a cheerful giver. And God is able to provide you with every blessing in abundance, so that you may always have enough of everything and may provide in abundance for every good work.

The contrast being made here is between being stingy in your financial support of the Church and being magnanimous. Obviously, God wants you to be in the latter category. Why? Not because *he* needs money—although the Church surely does—but rather because the more generous and cheerful you are in your giving, the more like him you become.

Think for a moment of all the good things God has generously lavished upon you in this life—including life itself! And think about that when the collection basket makes its way to your pew on Sunday. Give cheerfully and out of love for God.

Your generosity will unlock doors through which God can bring you closer to him. And spiritually you will be richer than in your wildest dreams.

HEBREWS 12:14

Strive for peace with all men, and for the holiness without which no one will see the Lord.

This scriptural truth could be expressed in the following simple syllogism:

1. Anyone who desires to see the Lord in heaven must be holy.
2. You desire to see the Lord in heaven.
3. Therefore, you must be holy.

Think about that.

I JOHN 2:1–6

My little children, I am writing this to you so that you may not sin; but if any one does sin, we have an advocate with the Father, Jesus Christ the righteous; and he is the expiation for our sins, and not for ours only but also for the sins of the whole world. And by this we may be sure that we know him, if we keep his commandments. He who says "I know him" but disobeys his commandments is a liar, and the truth is not in him; but whoever keeps his word, in him truly love for God is perfected. By this we may be sure that we are in him: he who says he abides in him ought to walk in the same way in which he walked.

This passage reminds us where the rubber meets the road when it comes to the gospel of Jesus Christ. He does not want us to merely pay lip service to his commandment to "love one another." We have to really *do* it. Our love must be real.

If you really love Jesus, you will love others for his sake and according to the way he commanded (see Matthew 25:31–46 for an example of what he said about this). To do anything less is to fall short of the goal the Lord has set for you.

CHAPTER 11
The Sanctity of Human Life

PSALM 127:3–5

Behold, sons are a heritage from the LORD,
    the fruit of the womb a reward.
Like arrows in the hand of a warrior
    are the sons of one's youth.
Happy is the man who has
    his quiver full of them!

In the late 1970s the television show *Eight Is Enough* became a hit. The title gave voice to the nearly universal negative attitude toward large families that had developed in the United States. Many people see having lots of children as repugnant, incomprehensible and financially impossible.

Sacred Scripture has a very different message. God tells us in this psalm that each and every child is a wonderful blessing, and having many children is a multiplication of blessings. Families who are open to life are living proof that this is true.

In Genesis 1:26–28, after God created Adam and Eve, he told them to "be fruitful and multiply." This does not mean, and the Catholic Church definitely does not teach, that married couples are obligated to crank out every last child they can possibly procreate. Rather, what God expects from all married couples is that they accept lovingly all children that God might choose to send them.

Saying yes to God without reservation may not result in the outcome you expect, but it will order your will to his will. In so doing you will become authentically free and find *real* happiness.[1]

PSALM 139:13—16

For you formed my inward parts,
    you knitted me together in my mother's womb.
I praise you, for I am wondrously made.
    Wonderful are your works!
You know me right well;
    my frame was not hidden from you,
when I was being made in secret,
    intricately wrought in the depths of the earth.
Your eyes beheld my unformed substance;
    in your book were written, every one of them,
the days that were formed for me,
    when as yet there was none of them.

One of the most astounding and impressive medical tools developed in recent years is ultrasound. This technology gives doctors the ability to view an unborn child at the early stages of development in amazingly detailed clarity.[2] It provides vivid evidence of the teaching of this passage.[3]

All one has to do is *see* the unborn child in the womb to recognize what God declared thousands of years ago in Scripture: The unborn baby is a human being. As more people start seeing this beautiful truth with their own eyes, the billion-dollar abortion industry will start to dry up. May God hasten that day!

ISAIAH 5:20—21

Woe to those who call evil good and good evil,
who put darkness for light
    and light for darkness,
who put bitter for sweet
    and sweet for bitter!
Woe to those who are wise in their own eyes,
    and shrewd in their own sight!

This passage stands as a stinging rebuke to Catholics who persist in their insanity of supporting abortion. It is truly sickening to see Catholic politicians brazenly proclaim that legal abortion is "good for women." They are indeed calling a grave evil "good."

Dr. Bernard Nathanson is one of many medical professionals who have had a radical change of heart concerning abortion. He presided over seventy-five thousand infant deaths in his medical practice, and he was one of the founders of the National Association for the Repeal of Abortion Laws (NARAL) in the United States. By the grace of God, he joined the pro-life cause and later the Catholic Church. He explained how pro-abortion extremists in government, media and elsewhere have pushed their deadly agenda:

> A truthful poll of opinion [in 1968] would have found that most Americans were against permissive abortion. Yet within five years we had convinced the U.S. Supreme Court to issue the decision which legalised abortion throughout America…and produced virtual abortion on demand up to birth. How did we do this? It is important to understand the tactics involved because these tactics have been used throughout the western world with one permutation or another, in order to change abortion law.
>
> The first key tactic was to capture the media. We persuaded the media that the cause of permissive abortion was a liberal enlightened, sophisticated one. Knowing that if a true poll were taken, we would be soundly defeated, we simply fabricated the results of fictional polls. We announced to the media that we had taken polls and that 60% of Americans were in favour of permissive abortion. This is the tactic of the self-fulfilling lie. Few people care to be in the minority. We aroused enough sympathy to sell our program of permissive abortion by fabricating the number of illegal abortions done annually in the U.S. The actual figure was approaching

100,000 but the figure we gave to the media repeatedly was 1,000,000. Repeating the big lie often enough convinces the public. The number of women dying from illegal abortions was around 200–250 annually. The figure we constantly fed to the media was 10,000. These false figures took root in the consciousness of Americans convincing many that we needed to crack the abortion law. Another myth we fed to the public through the media was that legalising abortion would only mean that the abortions taking place illegally would then be done legally. In fact, of course, abortion is now being used as a primary method of birth control in the U.S. and the annual number of abortions has increased by 1500% since legalisation.

The second key tactic was to play the Catholic Card. We systematically vilified the Catholic Church and its "socially backward ideas" and picked on the Catholic hierarchy as the villain in opposing abortion. This theme was played endlessly. We fed the media such lies as "We all know that opposition to abortion comes from the hierarchy and not from most Catholics" and "Polls prove time and again that most Catholics want abortion law reform". And the media drum-fired all this into the American people, persuading them that anyone opposing permissive abortion must be under the influence of the Catholic hierarchy and that Catholics in favour of abortion are enlightened and forward-looking. An inference of this tactic was that there were no non-Catholic groups opposing abortion. The fact that other Christian as well as non-Christian religions were (and still are) monolithically opposed to abortion was constantly suppressed.[4]

How's that for "calling evil good and good evil"?

Thanks be to God for Dr. Nathanson's conversion to the truth. Let us pray for the conversion of many others like him.

CHAPTER 12
Death, Judgment, Heaven and Hell

DEUTERONOMY 30:15—19

See, I have set before you this day life and good, death and evil.
If you obey the commandments of the LORD your God which
I command you this day, by loving the LORD your God, by
walking in his ways, and by keeping his commandments and his
statutes and his ordinances, then you shall live and multiply,
and the LORD your God will bless you in the land which you
are entering to take possession of it. But if your heart turns
away, and you will not hear, but are drawn away to worship
other gods and serve them, I declare to you this day, that you
shall perish; you shall not live long in the land which you are
going over the Jordan to enter and possess. I call heaven and
earth to witness against you this day, that I have set before you
life and death, blessing and curse; therefore choose life, that you
and your descendants may live.

Any of us old enough to remember black-and-white crime
movies have heard the challenge "Your money or your life!"
"What a no-brainer," we think, and quite correctly. Of *course* I'd
hand over my money if the choice were between it and my life.

But what if the choice were between your money and your
eternal life? Would you hand over your money in order to gain
the far greater riches of heaven?

God has given us each the freedom to choose to do what is
good or to do what is evil. In order for our love for him to be
genuine, it has to be freely given. God won't force you to love
and obey him, even though those are the two things that lead
directly to true happiness. What God *will* do is make you an

offer you can't refuse if you're seeing straight. He lays before each of us good and evil and asks us to choose, with the assistance of his grace, to do the good.

"Evil" in this context refers to choosing a lesser good (for example, food, sex, entertainment or material possessions) that is contrary to the will of God. Sexual pleasure, for example, is a created good that God permits to married couples but not to single people. So choosing sex outside of marriage is choosing evil.[1]

As Deuteronomy 30:15–19 tells us, the smart thing to choose is the good; this is the path to eternal life.

JOB 1:21

Naked I came from my mother's womb, and naked shall I return; the LORD gave, and the LORD has taken away; blessed be the name of the LORD.

Death is for good reason called "the great leveler." It doesn't matter who you are, how much money you have, how nice your house may be or how good your golf game is. Sooner or later you're going to die (see Hebrews 9:27). And when that day comes, nothing will accompany you into the afterlife: not money, not fame, not possessions, nothing.

So doesn't it make sense to recognize that, just as you came into this world relying totally on God for your very existence, you should leave relying totally on him? This is what's called "dying in the state of grace."

This passage is a helpful reminder that this earthly life is strictly temporary, and every good thing we have—including our very existence—depends completely upon God. Live your life with that truth clearly in view, and when death comes, you will enter eternal life blessing the name of the Lord.

PSALM 23:1—6

The LORD is my shepherd,
    I shall not want;
    he makes me lie down in green pastures.
He leads me beside still waters;
    he restores my soul.
He leads me in paths of righteousness
    for his name's sake.

Even though I walk through the valley of the
    shadow of death,
    I fear no evil;
for you are with me;
    your rod and your staff,
    they comfort me.

You prepare a table before me
    in the presence of my enemies;
you anoint my head with oil,
    my cup overflows.
Surely goodness and mercy shall follow me
    all the days of my life;
and I shall dwell in the house of the LORD
    for ever.

They say there are no atheists in foxholes. To borrow a line from Samuel Johnson, when a man knows he is about to die, "it concentrates his mind wonderfully."[2]

Psalm 23 has long been a comforting passage of Scripture for Jews and Christians in times of danger. And for good reason. As the psalmist declares, even though our path through life may lead through the valley of the shadow of death and eventually through the doorway of physical death, our good and loving God is with us each step of the way, restoring, comforting and protecting us and guiding us into unimaginable happiness with him forever.

EZEKIEL 18:22–32

If a wicked man turns away from all his sins which he has committed and keeps all my statutes and does what is lawful and right, he shall surely live; he shall not die. None of the transgressions which he has committed shall be remembered against him; for the righteousness which he has done he shall live.... But when a righteous man turns away from his righteousness and commits iniquity and does the same abominable things that the wicked man does, shall he live? None of the righteous deeds which he has done shall be remembered; for the treachery of which he is guilty and the sin he has committed, he shall die.

Yet you say, "The way of the Lord is not just." Hear now, O house of Israel: Is my way not just? Is it not your ways that are not just? When a righteous man turns away from his righteousness and commits iniquity, he shall die for it; for the iniquity which he has committed he shall die. Again, when a wicked man turns away from the wickedness he has committed and does what is lawful and right, he shall save his life. Because he considered and turned away from all the transgressions which he had committed, he shall surely live, he shall not die. Yet the house of Israel says, "The way of the Lord is not just." O house of Israel, are my ways not just? Is it not your ways that are not just?

Therefore I will judge you, O house of Israel, every one according to his ways, says the Lord GOD. Repent and turn from all your transgressions, lest iniquity be your ruin. Cast away from you all the transgressions which you have committed against me, and get yourselves a new heart and a new spirit! ... For I have no pleasure in the death of any one, says the Lord GOD; so turn, and live.

God's clear warning is that the wicked will bring permanent, eternal ruin upon themselves if they persist in their sins (see Ezekiel 3:18–21; Romans 2:1–11; Revelation 20:1–15). Yes, this is a grim and unpleasant message, but it's true, and it would be futile (not to mention stupid) to ignore it.

Remember that God's revelation to us is always in the form of "I have bad news and good news." The bad news of the danger of hellfire is accompanied by the Good News of mercy, forgiveness and salvation. God urges in this passage, "Turn and live!" The choice is ours.

MATTHEW 5:27–30

You have heard that it was said, "You shall not commit adultery." But I say to you that every one who looks at a woman lustfully has already committed adultery with her in his heart. If your right eye causes you to sin, pluck it out and throw it away; it is better that you lose one of your members than that your whole body be thrown into hell. And if your right hand causes you to sin, cut it off and throw it away; it is better that you lose one of your members than that your whole body go into hell.

We live in a pornographic culture. Erotic images intended to arouse us sexually are everywhere: on television, in the movies, in magazines and books, in advertisements of all types, on the Internet and so on. It's very hard to stay away from these images, and many people—men and women, boys and girls—are being swept into the vortex of sexual sin through what they see in pornography.

Consider these statistics of just how bad things have become in the United States: every *second* $3,075.64 is spent on pornography, 28,258 Internet users are viewing pornography, and 372 Internet users are typing adult search terms into search engines. And every thirty-nine minutes a new pornographic video is produced.[3]

It's no wonder that sins of the flesh abound. This generation, perhaps more than any other in human history, must heed these words about the dangers that arise from what we see.

The solution, while simple, is not easy. It's a practice known as "custody of the eyes," a form of mortification in which we carefully guard what we allow ourselves to look at. Catholic philosopher and author Joseph Pieper describes the practice and purpose of this discipline: "[Man] radically closes off the inner space of his life against the pressing of unruly pseudo-reality of empty sights and sounds—in order that…he might safeguard or recoup that which truly constitutes man's living existence: to perceive the reality of God and of creation and to shape himself and the world by the truth that discloses itself only in silence."[4]

MATTHEW 6:19–21

Do not lay up for yourselves treasures on earth, where moth and rust consume and where thieves break in and steal, but lay up for yourselves treasures in heaven, where neither moth nor rust consumes and where thieves do not break in and steal. For where your treasure is, there will your heart be also.

Here we come face-to-face with another ugly reality of our time: anxiety about money. Many Americans expend vast amounts of time and energy scrutinizing their stock portfolios, their bank balances and the resale value of their homes. Money has become an idol for many, a false god they both worship and are enslaved to.

Clearly these earthly things are all passing away. Even in this life we see them snatched away— by thieves, natural disaster and stock market convulsions. Whatever we have when we die, we leave behind. We enter eternity with nothing but ourselves, our sins and our love for God (or the lack of it).

Christ is not condemning the possession of wealth. Rather he is pointing out the kind of treasure we should be busy accumulating. If we are diligent in our duties toward God—truly seeking his will, loving and serving others selflessly, cultivating virtue and rooting out our vices—then we are rich beyond compare, laying up treasure in heaven.

MATTHEW 7:3—5

Why do you see the speck that is in your brother's eye, but do not notice the log that is in your own eye? Or how can you say to your brother, "Let me take the speck out of your eye," when there is the log in your own eye? You hypocrite, first take the log out of your own eye, and then you will see clearly to take the speck out of your brother's eye.

When you get an eyelash or a piece of grit stuck in your eye, your world immediately grinds to a halt. You'll stop whatever you are doing to attend to this painful irritant.

Christ uses the word *eye* here as a metaphor for one's inner self. Having something stuck in *this* eye is the equivalent of having pride, anger, greed, hardheartedness or some other evil disposition lodged in the heart. Imagine if everyone were as quick to drop everything and deal with their problems of the heart as they are to deal with an eyelash stuck in their eye. How different and happy the world would be!

Christ is telling us several important things in this passage, but two stand out as particularly necessary. First, be quick to notice your own "specks" and "logs." Make a good confession, and life will be so much more pleasant without those spitirual irritants.

Second, whatever your brother's or sister's fault may be—sometimes others' faults are real, and sometimes they exist only in your imagination—they are ultimately his or her problems to solve, not yours. Unless you have a genuine duty to offer correction (for example, if you are the person's parent or coach or religious superior), keep your nose out of the situation. It's between that person and God.

MATTHEW 7:21–27

Not everyone who says to me, "Lord, Lord," shall enter the kingdom of heaven, but he who does the will of my Father who is in heaven. On that day many will say to me, "Lord, Lord, did we not prophesy in your name, and cast out demons in your name, and do many mighty works in your name?" And then will I declare to them, "I never knew you; depart from me, you evildoers."

Every one then who hears these words of mine and does them will be like a wise man who built his house upon the rock; and the rain fell, and the floods came, and the winds blew and beat upon that house, but it did not fall, because it had been founded on the rock. And every one who hears these words of mine and does not do them will be like a foolish man who built his house upon the sand; and the rain fell, and the floods came, and the winds blew and beat against that house, and it fell; and great was the fall of it.

One can imagine the final astonishment of someone who talks an awful lot about God and truth but does not live according to the truth. As this Scripture passage indicates, that person is in for an extremely unpleasant surprise on the Day of Judgment. Prophesying in Christ's name, casting out demons, doing mighty deeds even—none of these things count for anything if they are done apart from Christ. What matters is "the obedience of faith" (Romans 1:5; 16:26; see 2:13).

MATTHEW 24:4—14

And Jesus answered them, "Take heed that no one leads you astray. For many will come in my name, saying, 'I am the Christ,' and they will lead many astray. And you will hear of wars and rumors of wars; see that you are not alarmed; for this must take place, but the end is not yet. For nation will rise against nation, and kingdom against kingdom, and there will be famines and earthquakes in various places: all this is but the beginning of the sufferings.

"Then they will deliver you up to tribulation, and put you to death; and you will be hated by all nations for my name's sake. And then many will fall away, and betray one another, and hate one another. And many false prophets will arise and lead many astray. And because wickedness is multiplied, most men's love will grow cold. But he who endures to the end will be saved. And this gospel of the kingdom will be preached throughout the whole world, as a testimony to all nations; and then the end will come."

Many generations of Christians have wondered if *they* were living in the end times. Two thousand years have come and gone since Christ spoke these words, and that long-awaited day of his glorious return has not arrived. So what are we to think of this passage?

No Christian should dismiss *any* part of Sacred Scripture as "irrelevant" or "unimportant"; there is an objective historical reality underlying the written Word. For example, the story of Adam and Eve in the Garden (see Genesis 1—3) unveils for us certain truths about the human fall from grace and communion with God.[5] Similarly, we need to hear Jesus' words, here and elsewhere, about the inevitable end of the world and the judgment of the nations (see Matthew 25:31–46). Jesus meant every word of what he said, and we would be foolish to ignore it.

ACTS 10:34–35

Peter…said, "Truly I perceive that God shows no partiality, but in every nation any one who fears him and does what is right is acceptable to him."

God is all just, yes, but he is also all *merciful*. As Saint Peter declares here, God looks mercifully upon all those who, through no fault of their own, are ignorant of the fullness of the truth and yet cooperate as well as they are able with the light God has given them. Although we cannot say for sure what someone's ultimate destiny will be, either heaven or hell, we can trust in God's loving mercy and pray that those who fear God and strive to obey him, even without a full knowledge of who he is, will have the opportunity to receive the fullness of the truth sometime before dying. May God's will be done. [6]

ROMANS 2:5–8

But by your hard and impenitent heart you are storing up wrath for yourself on the day of wrath when God's righteous judgment will be revealed. For he will render to every man according to his works: to those who by patience in well-doing seek for glory and honor and immortality, he will give eternal life; but for those who are factious and do not obey the truth, but obey wickedness, there will be wrath and fury.

Let's first pause to consider the aspect of hell presented in this passage. Saint Paul speaks about wickedness being repaid in due time with "wrath" and "fury." These grim reminders may even give you a secret satisfaction when you think about so-and-so getting what he deserves on that day! Well, look at what the great Catholic author Frank Sheed said about this:

> Less common, subtler, but if anything more dangerous is [the temptation] that can be found among many devoted Christians—a wholehearted acceptance of hell, an almost luscious *delight* in the invention of tortures to be inflicted by a raging God upon sinners (in whose number they themselves evidently are not). They will associate this with God's love, but in such a way that love has a meaning unrelated to any known among men.
>
> They tell a story in Scotland of a preacher describing the sufferings of the damned: These are up to their necks in boiling pitch; suddenly an angel swoops down with a scythe; they bury their heads in the pitch, emerge with their eyes streaming and gasp (I spare you the Scottish accent): "But, Lord, we didn't know." Then the Lord, bending over them "with infinite mercy and compassion," says, "Well, you know now."
>
> It is a jest, of course, an exaggeration. But the exaggeration is not wholly wild, and there is a streak of seriousness in the jest. It would be no gain to be right about hell and wrong about God. We must see both truths— hell's existence and God's love—together.[7]

Remember this Bible passage when someone tries to convince you that we are saved by "faith alone." Here we see another of Saint Paul's reminders that "God will repay every man according to his works." This does not mean, of course, that man can work his way to salvation—that is the heresy of Pelagianism, condemned by the Catholic Church repeatedly—but it does affirm the important role that good works done in grace have in Christ's plan of salvation. It's worth noting that the Greek word for "works" used here in Romans 2 is *ergoi*—the same word that appears in passages such as Ephesians 2:8-9, where

Paul explains that we are saved by grace through faith, not by our own works. We see, therefore, that Scripture does not have an "either/or" teaching with regard to human obedience to God's laws. Rather, it is "both/and."

ROMANS 12:1–2

I appeal to you therefore, brethren, by the mercies of God, to present your bodies as a living sacrifice, holy and acceptable to God, which is your spiritual worship. Do not be conformed to this world but be transformed by the renewal of your mind, that you may prove what is the will of God, what is good and acceptable and perfect.

We must live *in* the world, but Christ is calling us and helping us, with his grace, to not live *as* the world does (see John 15:19, 17:15–16). This is why Saint Paul stresses the need for Christians to be "transformed" into the image of Jesus Christ. This "renewal of...mind" draws us close to God by the cultivation of virtue and the eradication of vice. Our desire to do his will deepens, not because of rewards but simply because God himself wills it.

To the extent you are conformed to God here, you will be capable of enjoying eternal union with him in heaven. The converse, of course, is true: the more you conform to the world, the further you remove yourself from God. And if you go far enough in that horrific direction, you will eventually remove yourself from God's presence altogether and forever. That is what the Bible calls hell.

1 CORINTHIANS 3:10–16

According to the commission of God given to me, like a skilled master builder I laid a foundation, and another man is building upon it. Let each man take care how he builds upon it. For no other foundation can any one lay than that which is laid, which is Jesus Christ. Now if any one builds on the foundation with gold, silver, precious stones, wood, hay, straw—each man's work will become manifest; for the Day will disclose it, because it will be revealed with fire, and the fire will test what sort of work each one has done. If the work which any man has built on the foundation survives, he will receive a reward. If any man's work is burned up, he will suffer loss, though he himself will be saved, but only as through fire.

Do you not know that you are God's temple and that God's Spirit dwells in you?

If you were to die right now, would you be *perfectly* ready to see God face-to-face, perfectly clean and spotless and prepared for the unimaginable glory of the beatific vision?

Most likely your answer is no. Although you are (I hope) in the state of grace (see Romans 1:20) and destined for heaven, there may be inordinate attachments to sin and unforgiven venial sins that must be removed from your soul before you see God face-to-face. "Nothing unclean" can enter heaven (Revelation 21:27). Jesus emphasized this fact with his story about a wedding guest who was not dressed properly (Matthew 22:11–14).[8]

These passages are some of the scriptural monuments to the Catholic doctrine of purgatory, the process of purification that God performs on the soul after death.[9] Notice that Saint Paul describes a situation that takes place on "the day" the man is judged (see Hebrews 9:27). The works of his life are exposed to the fiery presence of God's all-consuming love (Hebrews 12:29). The bad works and the temporal effects due to sin are likened to highly flammable things like wood, hay and straw. The good works—the gold, silver and precious stones—are refined by the same fire and retained. This process involves *suffering*, and when it is completed, the soul has been purified, and the person is ready to enter into glory.

The text reminds us that the person "*will* be saved" (future tense), but that this will occur only after he or she has passed "through fire." The early Church fathers were very clear on this doctrine of purgatory, as it is taught in Sacred Scripture and handed down in Tradition from the Apostles. Saint Augustine wrote: "Temporal punishments are suffered by some in this life only, by some after death, by some both here and hereafter; but all of them before that last and strictest judgment."[10]

The Church teaches that we can pray for souls undergoing the fires of purgatory. Saint Augustine also wrote: "[T]he souls of the dead find relief through the piety of their friends and relatives who are still alive, when the Sacrifice of the Mediator (see 1 Timothy 2:5) is offered for them, or when alms are given in the church."[11]

JAMES 4:13–17

Come now, you who say, "Today or tomorrow we will go into such and such a town and spend a year there and trade and get gain"; whereas you do not know about tomorrow. What is your life? For you are a mist that appears for a little time and then vanishes. Instead you ought to say, "If the Lord wills, we shall live and we shall do this or that." As it is, you boast in your arrogance. All such boasting is evil. Whoever knows what is right to do and fails to do it, for him it is sin.

Life is unpredictable, and our bodies are fragile, susceptible to many dangers. So it is pure folly to assume that we will live forever or even for a long time. Only God knows.

Here God is telling us quite emphatically that we should live in a state of constant preparation for the day when our life will end. Then we will have no reason to fear death.

Think of the quarter million people who perished in the tsunami in southeast Asia on December 26, 2004. None of them were expecting death to come for them that day. Such occurrences serve as reminders to "have our house in order" at all times. Anything else is folly.

NOTES

INTRODUCTION

1. Jerome, *Commentariorum in Isaiam libri xviii*, prol.: J.P. Migne, *Patrologia Latina* (Paris, 1841–1855), 24, 17b.

CHAPTER 1: THE ONE TRUE GOD

1. Additional verses that speak about the divinity of Christ are John 1:1–2, 14; Romans 9:4–5; 1 Timothy 1:15–17; Titus 2:11–14; Hebrews 1:5–9; 2 Peter 1:1; 1 John 5:20. Compare Isaiah 43:10–12 and 44:6–7 with Revelation 1:17; 2:8 and 22:13.

2. The word *god* is used here in some translations, such as the *New American Bible*, but it does not refer to the one true God. The footnote to this verse in the *New American Bible* says:

   > *Little less than a god*: Hebrew *'elohim*, the ordinary word for "God" or "the gods" or members of the heavenly court. The Greek version translated *'elohim* by "angel, messenger"; several ancient and modern versions so translate. The meaning seems to be that God created human beings almost at the level of the beings in the heavenly world. Heb 2, 9 finds the eminent fulfillment of this verse in Jesus Christ, who was humbled before being glorified. Cf also 1 Cor 15, 27, where St. Paul applies to Christ the closing words of v 7.

3. A light year is a unit of measurement equal to the distance that light will travel in a vacuum in one year—365 twenty-four-hour days. Since light travels at about 186,282 miles per second, over the course of one year light will traverse about 5,878, 625, 373,183 miles. It is truly incomprehensible that the Hubble Telescope can detect images that are *billions* of light years away.

4. Mormonism practices polytheism with a particular slant of *henotheism*, which is the belief in a "chief" God who is above other gods.

5. This is a key example of how Mormons, although they make use of Christian terminology (that is, grace, salvation, heaven,

atonement and so forth), teach doctrines that are antithetical to Christianity, such as their rejection of the Trinity in favor of the notion that there are many gods and that the Father, Son and Holy Spirit are three separate and distinct gods. Taking notice of this serious theological defect in Mormonism, the Catholic Church has declared that Mormon baptisms are not valid (see Congregation for the Doctrine of the Faith, "Response to a 'Dubium' on the Validity of Baptism Conferred by The Church of Jesus Christ of Latter-day Saints, Called Mormons," June 5, 2001, www.vatican.va.)

CHAPTER 2: JESUS CHRIST, TRUE GOD AND TRUE MAN

1. Augustine provides a detailed and sophisticated discussion of the Christological implications of this passage in *De Trinitate* I:9, II:9, 27 and XV:19–20. See also Thomas Aquinas, *Summa Theologiae* I, Qq. 27–43.

2. Indeed, it is more proper to say that God *is* his existence, for being is not something that he *has*, but rather it is an aspect of his very essence. See Thomas Aquinas, *Summa Theologiae* I, Q. 3, art. 4.

3. Space limitations do not permit a discussion here of the very important question of the possibility of salvation for those who don't believe in Jesus Christ. For that discussion see Pope John Paul II, *Dominus Iesus*, available electronically at www.vatican.va.

4. The Greek word used here for image, *eikonos*, is the same word from which we derive the English word *icon*. In his battle against the iconoclastic heresy in the late eighth century, Saint John Damascene employed this passage in defense of the holy images and icons, which the iconoclasts were bent on eliminating from the Church. See the acts of the Second Nicene Council (AD 787), available electronically at http://www.fordham.edu.

5. This issue is part of the doctrine of divine appropriation. See Michael O'Carroll, *Trinitas: A Theological Dictionary of the Holy Trinity* (Wilmington, Del.: Glazier, 1987), p. 17.

CHAPTER 3: SALVATION

1. U.S. Census Bureau, "World Vital Events Per Time Unit: 2008," www.census.gov.

2. See Peter Kreeft, "The Fear of the Lord," *Envoy Magazine*, Vol. 7.5, pp. 24–25.

3. This touches on the "problem of evil," a dilemma of perennial concern to thinking people, who puzzle over how God can be both all-loving and all-powerful and yet allow evil in the world. The "problem" enters when the questions are raised: If God is all-loving, why does he allow such things to take place? If he is all-powerful, can't he stop them from happening? Peter Kreeft and Father Ronald Tacelli, S.J., have written a masterful Christian response to the problem of evil (and many other problems people have with God) in their excellent book *Handbook of Christian Apologetics: Hundreds of Answers to Crucial Questions* (Downers Grove, Ill.: Intervarsity Press, 1994).

4. See Augustine, *The Handbook on Faith, Hope, and Love* (*The Inchridion*), chapter 103; *City of God*, bk. 15, chap. 1, bk. 21, chap. 24.

5. See Council of Trent, session VI, chapter 8.

6. Contrary to a common Protestant error on this subject, God indeed *pours out* his grace on the justified sinner. "To pour out" means "to infuse." Scripture attests to the Catholic teaching on infused—as opposed to a strictly extrinsic, imputed grace—in passages such as Acts 2:17–18; 4:31; 6:8; 10:45; 11:24; Romans 5:5; Ephesians 5:18; Titus 3:5–7.

7. Author translation. *"Quod est ergo meritum hominis ante gratiam, quo merito percipiat gratiam, cum omne bonum meritum nostrum non in nobis faciat nisi gratia et cum Deus coronat merita nostra, nihil aliud coronet quam munera sua?"* (Epistle 154, 5:16).

8. This public debate, held in a Protestant church before an audience of some sixteen hundred people, titled "What Still Divides Us? A Catholic/Protestant Debate on *Sola Scriptura* and *Sola Fide*" (Patrick Madrid et al. versus Michael Horton et al.), is available in CD and in downloadable MP3 formats from Surprised by Truth Seminars, P.O. Box 640, Granville, OH 43023, www.surprisedbytruth.com.

9. See Council of Trent, session VI, canons 1–26.

CHAPTER 4: DIVINE REVELATION

1. Thomas Aquinas explained:

    > After quoting Genesis 1:26 ("Let us make man in our image, after our likeness") and St. Augustine ("Where an image *exists*, there forthwith is likeness; but where there is

likeness, there is not *necessarily* an image"), St. Thomas Aquinas explains that "likeness is *essential* to an image; and that an image adds something to likeness—namely, that it is copied from something else. For an 'image' is so called because it is produced as an imitation of something else; wherefore, for instance, an egg, however much like and equal to another egg, is not called an image of the other egg, because it is not copied from it.

"But equality does not belong to the *essence* of an image; for as *Augustine* says (QQ. 83): 'Where there is an image there is not *necessarily* equality,' as we see in a *person's* image reflected in a glass. Yet this is of the *essence* of a perfect image; for in a perfect image nothing is wanting that is to be found in that of which it is a copy. Now it is manifest that in *man* there is some likeness to *God*, copied from *God* as from an exemplar; yet this likeness is not one of equality, for such an exemplar *infinitely* excels its copy. Therefore there is in *man* a likeness to *God*; not, indeed, a perfect likeness, but imperfect. And *Scripture* implies the same when it says that *man* was made "to" *God's* likeness; for the preposition "to" signifies a certain approach, as of something at a distance" (*Summa Theologiae* Ia., Q. 93, art. 1).

2. John Paul II, *Veritatis Splendor* (Boston: St. Paul, 1993), p. 9.
3. In contrast to those who claim that it is impossible for human beings to please God by obeying his commandments (through corporal and spiritual good works) when assisted by his grace, see Luke 1:5–6; Romans 2:6–8, 13; Philippians 2:12–16; 1 Timothy 2:1–4.
4. For a more detailed discussion of this subject, see Patrick Madrid, "*Sola Scriptura*: A Blueprint for Anarchy," *Catholic Dossier*, March/April 1996.
5. See Vatican II, *Dei Verbum*, nos. 7–10.
6. Basil, *On the Holy Spirit*, chap. 27, no. 66, available at www.newadvent.org, emphasis added.
7. From John Chrysostom, *Homilies on Lazarus and the Rich Man*, trans. Kevin Perrotta and used with permission. Greek text in J.P. Migne, ed., *Patrologia Graeca*, vol. 48, columns 991–993. For a discussion of how many Protestants misunderstand and misuse this

passage in an attempt to support the Reformation notion of *sola scriptura*, see Patrick Madrid, "The White Man's Burden," *This Rock* Magazine, October 1993, available electronically at www.surprisedbytruth.com. See also the eight-CD audio set of the highly instructive Catholic Protestant debate on *sola scriptura* and *sola fide*, "What Still Divides Us?" available at www.patrickmadrid.com.

8. Saint Vincent of Lérins warned about the various groups of his own day (the early fifth century) who did this:

> Do heretics also appeal to Scripture? They do indeed, and with a vengeance; for you may see them scamper through every single book of Holy Scripture—through the books of Moses, the books of Kings, the Psalms, the Epistles, the Gospels, the Prophets. Whether among their own people, or among strangers, in private or in public, in speaking or in writing, at convivial meetings, or in the streets, hardly ever do they bring forward anything of their own which they do not endeavor to shelter under words of Scripture. Read the works of Paul of Samosata, of Priscillian, of Eunomius, of Jovinian, and the rest of those pests, and you will see an infinite heap of instances, hardly a single page, which does not bristle with plausible quotations from the New Testament or the Old. (*Commonitoria*, chap. 25, no. 64, available at www.newadvent.org).

9. For more on the subject of Tradition, see Yves Congar, *The Meaning of Tradition* (San Francisco: Ignatius, 2004); Patrick Madrid, *Why Is* That *in Tradition?* (Huntington, Ind.: Our Sunday Visitor, 2002).

10. For a good overview of this important issue of the canon of Scripture, see Gary Michuta, *Why Catholic Bibles Are Bigger: The Untold Story of the Lost Protestant Bible* (Chicago: Grotto, 2007); Henry Graham, *Where We Got the Bible: Our Debt to the Catholic Church* (San Diego: Catholic Answers, 2000).

CHAPTER 5: THE CHURCH

1. Mormons do not claim to know exactly when the alleged "Great Apostasy" took place, but they generally contend that it happened within about two hundred years of Christ's public ministry.

For example, the late Bruce McConkie, a prominent Mormon leader and theologian, in the 1958 edition of his popular book *Mormon Doctrine*, wrote explicitly about how the alleged universal apostasy began during the time of the Twelve Apostles and led to what are known as the Dark Ages. He claimed that this apostasy and moral darkness was universal. He identified the Catholic Church to be the corrupt, counterfeit organization that allegedly appeared on the scene after the demise of the true Church established by Christ (see McConkie's somewhat expurgated comments to this effect, with explicit mention of the Catholic Church removed, in *Mormon Doctrine* [Salt Lake City: Bookcraft, 1966], pp. 43–44). McConkie had earlier identified the Catholic Church as the "Great and Abominable" church that is described in the Book of Mormon (2 Nephi 28; Mormon 8:28–38; see also Joseph Smith, *Doctrine and Covenants* 10:56). Mormon apologist Michael R. Ash, for example, admits that McConkie said this about the Catholic Church. See his essay "Mormon Myths: Great and Abominable Church" (available electronically at www.mormonfortress.com), in which he quotes McConkie's 1958 edition of *Mormon Doctrine*: "It is also to the Book of Mormon to which we turn for the plainest description of the Catholic Church as the great and abominable church. Nephi saw this 'church which is the most abominable above all other churches' in [his] vision. He 'saw the devil that he was the foundation of it'" (*Mormon Doctrine*, 1958 ed., p. 130).

2. For an apologetics-related discussion of the issue of the infallibility of the Catholic Church, in particular the pope, see Patrick Madrid, *Pope Fiction: Answers to 30 Myths and Misconceptions About the Papacy* (San Diego: Basilica, 2000).

3. See also *CCC*, 865 and *The Catholic Encyclopedia*, "Unity (As a Mark of the Church)," available electronically at www.newadvent.org.

CHAPTER 6: EVANGELIZATION

1. For plenty of practical advice on this point, see Patrick Madrid, *Search and Rescue: How to Bring Your Family and Friends into, or Back into, the Catholic Church* (Manchester, N.H.: Sophia Institute, 2001).

2. Peter Kreeft, "Evidence for the Resurrection of Christ," http://peterkreeft.com.

3. See Pope John Paul II, *Veritatis Splendor*, nos. 90–94.

CHAPTER 7: THE SACRAMENTS

1. See Patrick Madrid, *Does the Bible Really Say That? Discovering Catholic Teaching in Scripture* (Cincinnati: Servant, 2006), pp. 113–116; also Patrick Madrid, *Answer Me This!* (Huntington, Ind.: Our Sunday Visitor, 2003), pp. 182–188.

2. See *The Didache* 14:3; Justin Martyr, *Dialogue With Trypho* 41; Irenaeus, *Against Heresies* 4:17:5; Saint Athanasius, *Fourth Festal Letter* 4.

3. See Michael W. Holmes, ed., *The Apostolic Fathers: Greek Texts and English Translations* (Grand Rapids, Mich.: Baker, 1992), pp. 246–247.

4. Holmes, p. 267.

5. Thomas Aquinas, as quoted in James Socias, *Handbook of Prayers* (Huntington, Ind.: Our Sunday Visitor, 1992), pp. 281, 283.

6. For a discussion of this, see Patrick Madrid, "Ark of the New Covenant," *This Rock* Magazine, December 1991, available electronically at www.catholic.com/thisrock.

7. For a general discussion of the issue of *sola scriptura*, see Patrick Madrid, *Answer Me This!* pp. 37–63; also the Catholic/Protestant debates "Does the Bible Teach *Sola Scriptura*?" (Patrick Madrid vs. James White) and "What Still Divides Us?" both available on CD and as downloadable MP3 files from Surprised by Truth, P.O. Box 640, Granville, OH, 43023, www.surprisedbytruth.com.

8. See Madrid, *Why Is That in Tradition?* pp. 165–169.

9. See Thomas Aquinas, *Summa Theologiae, Supplementum Tertia Partis*, Q. 77, art. 1; Q. 81, art. 4.

10. Vatican II, *Lumen Gentium*, no. 20; see *CCC*, 1555, 1087.

11. Adultery—which is at least the presumptive result of divorce and remarriage—is repeatedly condemned in Scripture. See passages such as Exodus 20:14; Leviticus 20:10; Deuteronomy 5:18; Proverbs 6:32; Malachi 3:5; Matthew 5:31–32; Mark 10:11–12; Luke 18:19–20; Romans 2:22; 7:2–3; 13:8–10; 1 Corinthians 7:10–11; Hebrews 13:4.

12. The late Father Nicholas Halligan, O.P., provides helpful examples of such impediments in his chapter on marriage in *The Sacraments and Their Celebration* (Mahwa, N.Y.: Alba, 1968), pp. 154–275. See also Pete Vere and Michael Trueman, *Surprised by Canon Law: 150 Questions Catholics Ask About Canon Law* (Cincinnati: Servant, 2004), pp. 113–119.

13. The Catholic Church affirms that children born to a man and woman whose legally recognized marriage was later declared sacramentally "null" (that is, they received a declaration of nullity from the Church) are legitimate (see 1983 *Code of Canon Law*, canons 1061, 1037). For a broader discussion of this issue, see the Web site of the diocese of Brooklyn, www.dioceseofbrooklyn.org.

14. Tertullian, as quoted by John Paul II, *Familiaris Consortio*, 13, www.vatican.va.

CHAPTER 8: THE COMMUNION OF SAINTS

1. See Patrick Madrid, *Any Friend of God's Is a Friend of Mine: A Biblical and Historical Explanation of the Catholic Doctrine of the Communion of Saints* (San Diego: Basilica, 1996), pp. 27–65.

2. For a fuller discussion of this issue, see Madrid, *Any Friend of God's Is a Friend of Mine*, pp. 17–66.

3. See Madrid, *Any Friend of God's Is a Friend of Mine,* pp. 43–65.

4. Alternative version, used in the Byzantine liturgy.

5. The word *sister*, as it was used by Jews in the time of Christ, could mean a sibling, niece, cousin or some other close family relation. More often than not, it did not mean "sibling."

6. Father Ronald Tacelli, s.j., provides a helpful discussion of the biblical evidence pointing to the perpetual virginity of Mary in his article "He's an Only Child," *Envoy* Magazine, vol. 1.3, available electronically at www.envoymagazine.com. For a detailed analysis of the patristic and medieval Fathers' teachings regarding the biblical evidence for Mary's perpetual virginity, see Luigi Gambero's two works *Mary and the Fathers of the Church: The Blessed Virgin Mary in Patristic Thought* (San Francisco: Ignatius, 1999) and *Mary in the Middle Ages: The Blessed Virgin Mary in the Thought of Medieval Latin Theologians* (San Francisco: Ignatius, 2005).

7. Today known in Arabic as *Banias*, this site lies close to the point where the borders of Syria, Lebanon and Israel meet, in the foothills of Mount Hermon, about a hundred miles north of Jerusalem.

8. For helpful information about this important biblical site, visit www.bibleplaces.com.

9. For a popular discussion of the early Church Fathers' comments on Simon Peter and his connection to this passage, see Madrid, *Why Is That in Tradition?* pp. 44–53; Madrid, *Pope Fiction*, pp. 37–50. Also

see Stanley L. Jaki, *And on This Rock* (Front Royal, Va.: Christendom, 1978).

10. See Madrid, *Pope Fiction*, pp. 31–33; Madrid, *Answer Me This!* pp. 105–122.

CHAPTER 9: TRIALS AND TEMPTATIONS

1. See Thomas Aquinas, *Summa Theologiae*, Ia–IIae, Q. 77, art. 1.

2. Teresa of Avila, "Lines Written in Her Breviary," in *Christian Prayer: The Liturgy of the Hours* (New York: Catholic Book, 1976), p. 1591.

3. The Council of Trent, "Decree on Justification," Session 6, chap. 13, in H.J. Schroeder, O.P., *Canons and Decrees of the Council of Trent: English Translation* (Rockford, Ill.: Tan, 1978), pp. 38–39.

4. John Chrysostom, *Homily 22 on Ephesians*, available electronically at www.newadvent.org.

5. For a series of helpful reflections on the causes and proper Christian response to the recent priest scandals, see Paul Thigpen, *Shaken by Scandals* (Charis, 2002).

CHAPTER 10: THE LAW OF LOVE

1. George J. Marlin, Richard P. Rabatin and John L. Swan, eds., *The Quotable Fulton Sheen: A Topical Compilation of the Wit, Wisdom, and Satire of Archbishop Fulton J. Sheen* (New York: Doubleday, 1989), p. 35.

2. See Hebrews 4:15, where it speaks of this in regard to how Christ was "tempted as we are, yet without sinning."

CHAPTER 11: THE SANCTITY OF HUMAN LIFE

1. Contraception and abortion are nothing other than a defiant *No!* in response to God's wise plan for married couples. The fact is, in marriages where contraception is practiced, many otherwise avoidable relationship problems develop, many times leading to the trauma of divorce. For specifics, visit the Couple to Couple League's Web site, http://ccli.org, and read true stories of couples who discovered what a disaster contraception is for marriage (see, for example, "Birth Control: It Almost Cost Us Our Marriage," by Bob and Gerri Laird).

2. For many amazing 4-D videos of babies in the womb, see www.windowtothewomb.co.uk.

3. "Professor Stuart Campbell at London's Create Health Clinic has perfected a technique which allows for the capture of 3-D records of foetal movements in the womb. Professor Campbell says that his new technique...'has been able to show for the first time that the unborn baby engages in complex behaviour from an early stage of its development.'

   Doctor Campbell has been able to capture many images of foetal behaviour, including a twelve week old foetus 'walking' in the womb, rubbing his/her eyes and yawning. These recordings disprove several previous held beliefs about foetal incapacities.

   Speaking about these new recordings John Smeaton, National Director of England's Society for the Protection of Unborn Children (SPUC), said: 'These pictures are a wonderful reminder of the fact that the unborn child is a living human being. These pictures are of babies as young as 12 weeks' gestation, the age at which a large percentage of abortions are carried out in this country. Tragically, unborn children such as these are killed at a rate of one every three minutes'" (LifeSiteNews.com, www.lifesitenews.com, quoting the BBC article "Scan Uncovers Secrets of the Womb," available at http://news.bbc.co.uk.).

4. Dr. Bernard Nathanson, "Confession of an Ex-abortionist," available electronically at www.aboutabortions.com and used by permission. See also "Sick of Death: The Testimony of Bernard Nathanson," *Boston Herald*, 1998, available electronically at www.catholiceducation.org.

CHAPTER 12: DEATH, JUDGMENT, HEAVEN AND HELL

1. See Thomas Aquinas, *Summa Theologiae*, Ia–IIae., Q. 2.

2. What the famously astute Dr. Johnson (1708–1784) actually said was less mellifluous but no less insightful: "Depend upon it, sir, when a man knows he is to be hanged in a fortnight, it concentrates his mind wonderfully." www.samueljohnson.com.

3. Family Safe Media, Pornography Statistics, available at http://familysafemedia.com.

4. Joseph Pieper, *A Brief Reader on the Virtues of the Human Heart* (San Francisco: Ignatius, 1991), p. 41.

5. See Pope Pius XII, *Humani Generis*, no. 37, www.vatican.va.

6. See Peter Kreeft, "The Fear of the Lord," *Envoy* Magazine, vol. 7.5, pp. 24–25.

7. F.J. Sheed, *Theology for Beginners* (Ann Arbor: Servant, 1981), p. 165, emphasis added.

8. Catholic Scripture scholar Bernard Orchard, O.P., explains this parabolic incident: "[T]he 'wedding-garment' is an allegorical element representing fitness for the kingdom; lack of such fitness is obviously culpable and requires no explanation. The man has no excuse to offer. The king passes sentence and the banquet begins or rather is resumed under new conditions, *i.e.*, it now becomes a banquet in which all are perfect" (*A Catholic Commentary on Holy Scripture* [London: Thomas Nelson and Sons, 1953], p. 890).

9. The man spoken of in 1 Corinthians 3 is like "one pulled out of a burning house, scorched but alive. The unworthy teacher will not lose his soul (he is not therefore guilty of mortal sin) but will lose his work and his special reward. The last words clearly imply some penal suffering, and as Paul connects it so closely with God's judgement, it can hardly be confined to suffering in this world, but seems to include the idea of purificatory suffering after this life, *i.e.*, in purgatory" (*A Catholic Commentary on Holy Scripture*, p. 1087).

10. Augustine continues:

    > But not all who suffer temporal punishments after death will come to eternal punishments, which are to follow after that judgment.... The prayer either of the Church herself or of pious individuals is heard on behalf of certain of the dead, but it is heard for those who, having been regenerated in Christ, did not for the rest of their life in the body do such wickedness that they might be judged unworthy of such mercy, nor who yet lived so well that it might be supposed they have no need of such mercy. (*The City of God* 21:13, in W.A. Jurgens, trans., *The Faith of the Early Fathers*, vol. 3 (Collegeville, Minn.: Liturgical, 1979), p. 106)

And in *Handbook on Faith, Hope, and Love* he writes:

> That there should be some such fire even after this life
> is not incredible, and it can be inquired into and either
> be discovered or left hidden whether some of the faith-
> ful may be saved, some more slowly and some more
> quickly in the greater or lesser degree in which they
> loved the good things that perish, through a certain
> purgatorial fire....
>
> The time which interposes between the death of a
> man and the final resurrection holds souls in hidden
> retreats, accordingly as each is deserving of rest or of
> hardship, in view of what it merited when it was living
> in the flesh. Nor can it be denied that the souls of the
> dead find relief through the piety of their friends and rel-
> atives who are still alive, when the Sacrifice of the
> Mediator is offered for them, or when alms are given in
> the church. But these things are of profit to those who,
> when they were alive, merited that they might afterward
> be able to be helped by these things. For there is a certain
> manner of living, neither so good that there is no need
> of these helps after death, nor yet so wicked that these
> helps are of no avail after death. (*Handbook on Faith,
> Hope, and Love* 18:69; 29:109, in Jurgens, pp. 149, 152)

11. Augustine, *Handbook on Faith, Hope, and Love*, 29:109, in Jurgens,
    p. 152.